• Britain's Scenic Railways •

Dawlish

The Railway from Exeter to Newton Abbot

Colin J. Marsden

Ian Allan
PUBLISHING

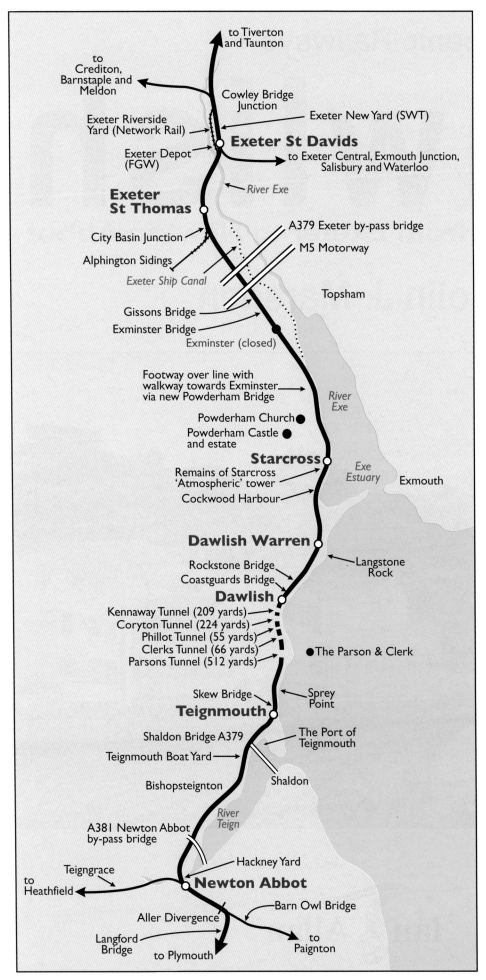

to Tiverton and Taunton

to Crediton, Barnstaple and Meldon

Cowley Bridge Junction

Exeter New Yard (SWT)

Exeter Riverside Yard (Network Rail)

Exeter St Davids

Exeter Depot (FGW)

to Exeter Central, Exmouth Junction, Salisbury and Waterloo

River Exe

Exeter St Thomas

City Basin Junction

A379 Exeter by-pass bridge

Alphington Sidings

M5 Motorway

Exeter Ship Canal

Topsham

Gissons Bridge

Exminster Bridge

Exminster (closed)

Footway over line with walkway towards Exminster via new Powderham Bridge

River Exe

Powderham Church

Powderham Castle and estate

Starcross

Remains of Starcross 'Atmospheric' tower

Exe Estuary

Exmouth

Cockwood Harbour

Dawlish Warren

Rockstone Bridge

Langstone Rock

Coastguards Bridge

Dawlish

Kennaway Tunnel (209 yards)

Coryton Tunnel (224 yards)

Phillot Tunnel (55 yards)

Clerks Tunnel (66 yards)

Parsons Tunnel (512 yards)

The Parson & Clerk

Skew Bridge

Sprey Point

Teignmouth

Shaldon Bridge A379

The Port of Teignmouth

Teignmouth Boat Yard

Bishopsteignton

Shaldon

River Teign

A381 Newton Abbot by-pass bridge

Hackney Yard

Teigngrace

to Heathfield

Newton Abbot

Barn Owl Bridge

Aller Divergence

Langford Bridge

to Plymouth

to Paignton

Front Cover: *Looking down at the Dawlish seafront from close to Kennaway Tunnel on 26 June 2010, a 2+7 CrossCountry Trains HST set, led by Class 43 No. 43303 with No. 43384 on the rear, forms the 07.00 Glasgow Central to Plymouth service.* **CJM**

Rear Cover: *One of the more picturesque views of trains traversing the scenic railway through Dawlish in South Devon is from the station footbridge, looking towards the west, where trains can be seen emerging from Kennaway Tunnel. On 3 March 2015, 'Building a Greater West' - liveried Class 43 No. 43144 leads train 1A81, the 08.44 Penzance to Paddington, seen traveling alongside Marine Parade.* **CJM**

Title Page: *Aggregate Industries-liveried Class 59/0 No. 59005 Kenneth J Painter emerges slowly from Kennaway Tunnel on 9 September 2013 and heads towards Dawlish station powering train 6Z27, the 11.13 Burngullow ECC yard to Exeter Riverside. The train should have been loaded with sand, but due to wagon contamination it was returned empty to Westbury. This was one of the rare occasions that a Class 59/0 has operated along the sea wall.* **CJM**

Front Endpaper *Dawlish woke up to a covering of the white stuff on 18 December 2010, one of the very rare occasions. The snowfall was heavier in other parts of the country and some minor disruption to rail services was experienced. However, CrossCountry Trains managed to get the 06.10 Derby to Plymouth through Dawlish just four minutes late, formed of 'Voyager' set No. 220027.* **CJM**

Rear Endpaper *In 2007, a number of empty First Great Western Mk3 HST rakes were loco-hauled along the Sea Wall en route to and from refurbishment which took place at Bombardier sites in Derby and Ilford. GBRf held the contract for these moves and Class 66s were used displaying a number of different liveries. On 27 July 2007 Metronet/GBRf-liveried No. 66718 Gwyneth Dunwoody passes below Rockstone (Black) Bridge with train 5Z90, the 09.03 Laira depot Plymouth to Bombardier Ilford. The train was formed of vehicles 9481 (barrier), 42318 (in Midland Main Line colours), 42299, 42298, 42099, 41140, 41139, 44037, 40715, and barrier 6721.* **CJM**

First published 2016

ISBN 978 0 7110 3838 7

Published by Ian Allan Publishing Ltd, Addlestone, Surrey KT12 2SF.

Printed in Bulgaria

Visit the Ian Allan Publishing website at www.ianallanpublishing.com

CONTENTS

Below: *Skirting the King's Walk between Dawlish station and Kennaway Tunnel, the Great Western Railway green-liveried HST set formed with power cars Nos. 43187 and 43188 with LA15 coaching stock set heads west on 30 September 2015 forming the 10.06 Paddington to Penzance service.* **CJM**

Britain's Scenic Railways Dawlish - The Railway from Exeter to Newton Abbot

DRS Class 37/6s Nos. 37607 and 37610 operate in 'top and tail' mode with a three vehicle Network Rail test train on 13 June 2014. The train is seen approaching Dawlish station, viewed from the station footbridge, and forms test special 1Z03, the 03.43 Plymouth to Bristol Barton Hill and Hither Green via Looe. **CJM**

INTRODUCTION

It is without doubt that the most photographed and followed section of railway line in the UK is the 21-mile (34km) route between Exeter and Newton Abbot, which en route traverses the world famous Dawlish and Teignmouth sea wall sections.

Since the publication of my two previous titles covering this scenic railway route, the sea wall hit world news on 5 February and again on 14 February 2014 when massive storms washed away a huge section of it at Dawlish and ripped apart the fabric of the line all the way from Dawlish Warren through to Teignmouth. This storm and its damage led to the closure of the line between Exeter and Newton Abbot for eight weeks, the longest closure due to weather damage since the line opened in the mid-1800s.

At the time of the Great 2014 Storm, as it has become known, I was in Canada on a photographic safari and saw the images on their morning TV news programme; it is quite concerning to see images of your home town being literally washed away from several thousand miles away. Thankfully I had returned to Dawlish before the second storm struck and was able to document the effects and repair work.

The entire route from Exeter to Newton Abbot passes through some of the most beautiful countryside in the country, from Exeter skirting the River Exe, passing the picturesque Powderham Estate and the photogenic Cockwood Harbour before traversing the stunning Dawlish Sea Wall section between Langstone Rock and Lea Mount in Dawlish. The line then dives in and out of five tunnels before travelling along the Teignmouth Sea Wall, then passes through the town of Teignmouth and skirts the River Teign before arriving at Newton Abbot, passing Newton Abbot race course and the site of the once extensive Newton Abbot depot and workshops.

Today, we see train services operated by Great Western Railway and CrossCountry Trains working along the Dawlish Sea Wall, bringing a mix of mainly HST, 'Voyager' and DMU classes, with the sleeper service from London to Penzance still being loco hauled.

Freight traffic along the sea wall is very sparse, with just a handful of booked trains each week; engineers trains, extra freights and departmental trains add to the enjoyment, with a good cross-section of train types and motive power classes seen over the route.

Over the years little had changed over the 21-mile line in terms of the rail route, except for significant erosion of the soft sandstone cliffs. However, the villages and towns have hugely enlarged, which is quite noticeable if old and new images are compared.

This title has been put together to show the route, development, train types and difficulties of running a sea wall railway, and in a special section covers the dramatic events of February 2014 and the following repair work.

I hope readers and viewers will enjoy their journey along one of Britain's most scenic railways between Exeter and Newton Abbot.

Colin J. Marsden
Dawlish, February 2016

Above: *A pair of UK Rail Leasing Class 56s Nos. 56104 and 56098 power Rail Operations Group train 5M56, the 11.00 Laira to Brush, Kilmarnock towards Dawlish station from Kennaway Tunnel on 8 November 2015. The train is formed of vehicles 6338, 40809, 42261, 44030, 42344, 42216, 41126, 42268, 42056 and 6330. The HST stock was en-route tor refurbishment.* **CJM**

ACKNOWLEDGEMENTS

The Author would like to thank the many people who have contributed to the production of this title. A special thank you is due to the contributing photographers who have provided some of the illustrations. Also a thank you must go to the many local people who have provided personal memories and recollections, and to many retired and serving railway staff who have answered countless, often trivial questions about the local area and its rail operation.

Finally I would like to thank Keith Ewins, Kevin Wills, Antony Christie, Nathan Williamson, Simon Thurgood, Sharon Watkins and Russel Watkins for their assistance. Lastly I would like to thank the proprietors of The Marine Tavern public house, Hillary Stanley and Andy Sharples, for providing much welcome liquid refreshment during the evenings and providing an excellent meeting house at which to talk about railways, trains and photographs.

Railways along the Sea Wall

This title covering the UK scenic railway along the South Devon coast through Dawlish and Teignmouth starts its journey at Cowley Bridge Junction, east of the main station in Exeter, that of Exeter St Davids, where the former London & South Western Railway (L&SWR), later Southern Railway, route to the west diverged from the former Great Western Railway (GWR) main line serving Exeter St Davids from the Taunton direction.

Today, this is a two-track (one 'up' and 'one' down) railway, operated by Network Rail with passenger train services operated by Great Western Railway and CrossCountry Trains, owned by Arriva Trains, a part of the German-owned Deutsche Bahn (DB) group.

The line east from Exeter St Davids was first opened in 1844 as part of the Bristol & Exeter Railway. The L&SWR route arrived in 1851. Access to and from the Crediton and north Devon line at Cowley Bridge is now via a ladder crossing arrangement, but originally this was a double junction. The area around Cowley Bridge Junction adjacent to the River Exe is prone to flooding and on many occasions has seen the line closed. Floods in recent years have led to Network Rail raising the height of electric control boxes to avoid water ingress, as well as the installation of a water protecting plastic and rubber boom which can be erected quickly if needed.

Just to the west of Cowley Bridge Junction is access to Exeter Riverside Yard; this yard was very busy with commercial freight up until the 1990s and then fell into decay. Today, it is used for the off-loading of ballast trains from the Mendips on a frequent basis, recessing of some DB-S freight services en route from the South West to South Wales and the Midlands, as well as the loading of infrequent log trains en route to the Kronospan wood processing plant in Chirk, North Wales. These trains are operated by Colas Rail Freight.

When Network Rail track and infrastructure test trains visit the West Country, these frequently stable in Exeter Riverside Yard. Today, the sizeable yard looks a mess, with the entire site weed infested, covered in heaps of ballast and piles of logs; the Great Western goods transfer shed is now in decay, and looks ready for demolition.

On the 'down' side of the running lines, closer to Exeter St Davids station, is Exeter West Yard; this two-track yard is used by South West Trains to stable Class 158 or 159 stock in use on services using the Waterloo route.

At the London end of Exeter St Davids station is Red Cow level crossing; this is a very busy road linking Exeter with the Exwick residential area. The single-barrier full-width gates are controlled by Exeter Power Signal Box, but a crossing keeper is retained to locally control pedestrian traffic. A fascinating line indicator is located adjacent to the crossing which, when a signal is cleared for a move over the crossing, sounds a bell and the track number and direction is displayed; this is visible from the pedestrian walkway.

Huge rationalisation of the Exeter St Davids area took place in

Right Below: *The view looking over Dawlish from the highest point of Lea Mount. Recorded on 1 May 1969, before a lot of development had taken place in the town, a pair of Class 42 'Warship' locos, Nos. D822* Hercules *and D827* Kelly, *head west with train 1C60, the 14.30 Paddington to Penzance.* **Bernard Mills**

Filmstrip Top Right: *Views of old Dawlish from Lea Mount.* **CJM-C**

Below: *On 15 June 2015, the first of a new freight flow commenced operation along the South Devon main line, with what should become a daily sand train from Burngullow in Cornwall to Bow in east London. The train operates west as one block train, but the loaded train has to work as two shorter (lighter weight) trains over the arduous Devon banks. One portion of the first train, the 12.53 Burngullow to Exeter Riverside, is seen passing Powderham headed by DB-S red/grey liveried Class 66 No. 66118.* **CJM**

the mid-1980s as part of the West of England resignalling project, which culminated in the two lines furthest away from the main station building becoming the 'up' and 'down' Great Western lines, while those closer to the station amenities became the Waterloo-bound lines, which are also used for GWR local services.

station furniture, the facility

Adjacent to Exeter St Davids station is Exeter motive power depot; over the years this has seen many uses from providing power to operate local services in the 1950s-70s, stabling local multiple unit stock, servicing locos used on the Waterloo to Exeter route, and servicing shunting locos used in the local area. After many suggestions of closure, the facility is now fully refurbished and much enlarged and is the principal First Great Western DMU depot in the West Country. In 2015 it was officially the home of eight Class 143 and 26 Class 15x DMMUs used through Devon and Cornwall. In 2015 further extensive refurbishment was ongoing. In addition to looking after the FGW DMMU stock, the depot also refuels the Network Rail locos visiting the area and if required can refuel main-line locomotives operating for Freightliner or Colas Rail Freight in the area.

Located at the west end of Exeter St Davids station is Exeter Power Signal Box, built in the 1980s as part of the West of England resignalling project. This modernised facility controls the lines from a point between Bridgwater and Cogload Junction on the Bristol route, Athelney on the route towards Castle Cary, Crediton on the Barnstaple/Meldon route, Exeter St James Park on the line to Exmouth/Honiton, Paignton, and to a point just west of Totnes on the main line.

West from Exeter St Davids the line departs the city on an embankment heading towards the suburb of St Thomas; this is a two-track section. Exeter St Thomas station is just a shadow of its former status with an overall roof; today it has 'bus-stop' type

is dirty, unwelcoming and offers no disabled access. West of Exeter St Thomas the remnants of the junctions for Exeter City Basin and Alphington spur which once formed the connection with the Teign Valley line to Chudleigh and Newton Abbot, closing in 1958, can be found. The Alphington line currently serves a scrap dealership, which sees an infrequent loaded DB-S scrap train operate to Cardiff.

From Exeter St Thomas, the twin-track route winds through the Exeter residential and industrial areas towards Exminster, and passes the large non-rail-connected Exeter waste disposal centre, before reaching and passing under Matford bridge and the M5 bridge just before the former Exminster station, closed in 1964, is reached. Plans currently exist for a new station to be built near Marsh Barton business park with a possibility of a further new station at Exminster.

Exminster sported both 'up' and 'down' loops until the 1980s West of England resignalling; these were very useful for the recessing of freight traffic, but as this has now declined to just a couple of trains per week, such luxuries are no longer offered.

After Exminster the line runs between the River Exe and the Powderham Estate, past the site of the steam era Exminster water troughs. After passing Powderham Castle, the home of the Earl of Devon, which can be clearly seen from passing trains, the line heads towards Starcross. Again, this is a one 'up' one 'down' station with very limited facilities, serving the local community as well as a summer-only ferry connection to Exmouth. Today, the station buildings are largely gone, with just 'bus-stop' facility. Part of the

station building has been taken over for retail use, currently a fish and chip shop. A footbridge crossing the line here offers excellent views of the line, the original Brunel Railway Atmospheric railway engine house building and the Exe estuary.

The route between Exeter and Teignmouth was first opened on 30 May 1846 and was extended to Newton Abbot in December the same year, this used Broad Gauge (7ft 0¼in) track. It was operated using atmospheric propulsion between 23 February and 20 September 1848, from when it was converted to conventional steam propulsion. The section was converted to standard gauge, 4ft 8½in, from 1892.

Just to the west of Starcross is the village of Cockwood together with the world famous Cockwood Harbour; without any doubt this is one of the most photographed locations on the Exeter to Newton Abbot route, and possibly in the world.

The small village of Cockwood sports two high-quality public houses, The Ship Inn and The Anchor; both offer excellent food and drink, but the village has few other amenities.

The railway crosses over the harbour on a causeway, which originally had three bridge openings to allow small craft into an inner harbour. However, only two remain today. The water side of the causeway is the Exe Estuary, which accommodates hundreds of river and sea craft and is a popular sailing area.

Since the railway route first opened in 1846, embankments on both sides of the harbour have provided excellent photographic vantage points for trains in both directions, depending on the time of day. However, in late 2007 Network Rail, for reasons of safety, erected a steel fence along the top of the causeway effectively ruining all subsequent photographs; bushes have now also grown up, spoiling the view.

The route, consisting of one 'up' and one 'down' line, follows the main A379 road between Starcross and Cockwood Harbour. The line, after crossing the water and harbour, then follows a back road to Dawlish via Cofton, Eastdon and Dawlish Warren; this provides some good vantage points of the line, especially during the afternoon. A public foot crossing is located adjacent to the small village of Cofton, which provides access to the foreshore at low tide and gives a photographic view of the line, but be careful as you are very close to the line.

It is of interest that, when standing in the Cockwood area, and looking east towards Exeter, trains can be seen on the Exeter to Exmouth line (once part of the Southern Railway network to East Devon, but now the stub end of the 'Avocet' branch line from Exeter).

The area around Starcross, Cockwood and towards Dawlish Warren is a special location in terms of wildlife. The estuary is designated as a Special Protection Area and a Site of Special Scientific Interest, as well as being an internationally important location for wintering waterfowl, and Divers, Grebes and Sea Ducks can be seen off the beach with many Waders such as Curlew, Avocets, Oystercatchers, Godwits, Dunlin and Ringed Plovers around the Estuary. It is also a stop off for birds such as Ospreys, Terns and other migrants. The Warren also has the rare Sand Lizard in the dunes as well as being an important area for plants such as the rare Sand (Warren) Crocus.

People wishing to visit Cockwood will experience very restricted parking on both sides of the harbour; however, good public transport is provided by Stagecoach Devon with their route No. 2 and the 2B from Exeter to Newton Abbot passing along the main road.

The area of the sea wall usually known as Dawlish Warren did not have a station until the summer of 1905 when a small halt, named Warren Halt, with platforms just 150ft (45.72m) long was opened. Due to growth and the desire to stop longer trains, these were extended a year later to 400ft (121.92m) in length. In 1907 small offices were added and the station was renamed Warren Platform. These facilities were not located at the site of the present Dawlish Warren station, but adjacent to the Great Western Railway footbridge which crosses the line between the car park at Dawlish Warren and the sea wall leading to Langstone Rock.

It was not until 1 October 1911 that the station was renamed Dawlish Warren. It was soon found to be inadequate for patronage, and a new station located on loop lines was opened on 23 September 1912. This facility had platforms 600ft (182.88m) in

Top: A panoramic view of Dawlish, taken from the breakwater. On the far left is Lea Mount and Kennaway Tunnel, the Colonnade Viaduct is just to the right of centre and Dawlish Warren and Langstone is on the far right. **CJM**

Right: About to dive into the 209 yard (191m) long Kennaway Tunnel and skirting the residential properties of Marine Parade, Dawlish, Freightliner Class 66/6 No. 66620 powers the 06.53 Westbury Cement Works to Moorswater loaded cement train on 18 May 2010. **CJM**

length and was located a quarter of a mile on the Exeter side of the original structure.

The new station sported buildings on both the 'up' and 'down' side, with vehicular access on the 'up' side. The station buildings on the 'down' side were destroyed by fire on 9 January 1924 and not replaced. A signal box was located at the Exeter end of the westbound platform, which opened when the loop lines were built in 1911 and remained in use until the West of England resignalling in 1986. A footbridge was provided between 'up' and 'down' platforms, but this was removed in the 1980s, meaning passengers have to use an unnatractive underbridge between the sides of the station. Part of the removed footbridge deck was later reused near Torre on the Newton Abbot to Paignton line to replace an ageing structure.

A small goods yard was located at the country end of the revised Dawlish Warren station and within its confines a camping coach was positioned from the summer of 1935, but by 1940 it was removed.

After a short period, public camping coaches were located on the site between 1942 and 1953 and by the summer of 1959 nine bogie carriages were available. In 1964 the British Railways (Western Region) camping coach service was withdrawn, with the carriages at Dawlish Warren taken over by the BR Staff Association. The original GW-design vehicles were worn out by 1982 and replaced by rebuilt Mk 1s and inspection saloons, which were prepared by Swindon Works and positioned in the old goods yard. Today these are operated privately, are in an appalling external condition and are rapidly becoming an eyesore.

The operational goods yard at Dawlish Warren remained with diminishing receipts until August 1967 when it closed. In 1971 the

station became unstaffed and today remains little more that a halt; not even a ticket issuing machine is provided.

With loop platforms for stopping trains, Dawlish Warren was frequently used to allow fast or main line services to overtake slower services or freight trains. The buildings on the 'up' side were, after closure, used to house the Dawlish Warren Railway Museum, but this closed in 1984 and the buildings were converted to holiday accommodation. Sadly the structure was destroyed by fire on the night of 15 June 2003. In 2007/08 a new structure, of like design to Dawlish Warren GW signal box, was built on the site of the original 'up' side buildings.

A walkway exists along the side of the railway the entire way from Dawlish Warren to Dawlish. The path is accessed from either the sea front or the original railway footbridge and leads along to Langstone Rock, also known as 'Red Rock'.

The area around Langstone Rock offers some outstanding views of trains in both directions, rounding the tight curve at the foot of the rock. It is possible to climb to the top of Langstone Rock, but by 2015 the badly eroding steps were becoming something of a problem; however, several small hills at the base of the rock are still available.

No amenities had ever existed on the sea wall, but in the late 1990s a small cafe took over the lease of a building at the foot of Langstone Rock and opened this as the Red Rock Cafe. This now has a thriving trade in hot and cold food and drinks. It is very enthusiast-friendly and is acknowledged by a high proportion of the trains that pass. It is a frequent meeting point for rail enthusiasts and is a hive of activity when steam trains operate.

Access to the amenities at Dawlish Warren, including the golf club, have always been a problem, as the rail overbridge at the country end of Dawlish Warren station has insufficient headroom to allow anything through but a car or small van, therefore fire engines and the like do not have full access to the Warren area. Various considerations have been given to allowing special vehicles access over the tracks, but this would require sophisticated interlocking with signalling, and would be a costly option. Following the 2014 sea wall collapse, the car park at Dawlish Warren became a major work site and occupation access was provided onto the track for road/rail vehicles. It is of course an emergency access to the railway.

The Dawlish Sea Wall between Dawlish Warren and Dawlish emerged as part of the construction of the rail line west from Exeter by the South Devon Railway in the mid-1840s to protect the line from the ravages of the sea. The line to Dawlish opened on 30 May 1846. Originally it was a single broad gauge track (7ft 0¼ in) operated by atmospheric pressure until September 1848. From its opening, the wall which was built progressively from 1836, located between the rail track and beach, was available for walkers between the two points and provided access to the increasingly popular bathing beaches.

In the main the wall was built at track height, except for a section

in 1901 and the building together with adjacent cottages became residential. In recent years the Coastguard building has been a restaurant and bar, while the boat house has been used for hiring out small water craft, but both were closed in 2008. The Coastguard building is now a private residence. A footbridge from the beach served the Coastguard structure and provided further access to the Exeter Road.

Dawlish station has by its position been the subject of many wash-outs over the years, with on numerous occasions parts of the 'down' platform station fencing and even parts of the station buildings being washed away.

Dawlish station boasted a busy goods yard, located on the 'up' side from the station's opening until 17 May 1965. The site was rebuilt as a car park, with office and workshop facilities for Network Rail and its contractors located at the London end which provided a messy scene for the visitor.

Directly west of Dawlish station the railway crosses the picturesque Colonnade Viaduct, which takes the line over a walkway to the sea wall and over Dawlish Water (The Brook), which divides the east and west sides of the town. The railway continues skirting Marine Parade to the first of five tunnels, Kennaway. The sea wall footpath continues on the sea side and from here to Kennaway Tunnel and Boat Cove is officially known as the King's Walk. Originally a wrought iron, now a steel and concrete, footbridge crosses the tracks at the portal of Kennaway Tunnel.

At this point the railway passes under Lea Mount, a tall land mass on which a number of footpaths exist, allowing walkers to climb the hill and gain excellent views of Lyme Bay and the railway all the way from Dawlish Warren (Langstone Rock).

The other four tunnels travelling west are Coryton, Phillot, Clerks and Parsons, the latter emerging onto the Teignmouth Sea Wall. Single-line operation remained through the five tunnels west of Dawlish until 1902-05 when full double-track operation was introduced; this delay was due to the amount of civil engineering required to increase the tunnel openings, which in several cases required the surrounding embankments to be shored up and major excavation work.

From the top of Lea Mount Gardens a good view of trains between the tunnels can be obtained, but this is quickly becoming overgrown.

A coastal path walkway exists between Dawlish and Teignmouth with a footpath over fields from near Old Teignmouth Road. This used to allow stunning views of trains emerging from Clarks Tunnel at Horse Cove, but sadly in recent years Network Rail have fenced this area in and photography is no longer possible.

After emerging from the 512 yard (468m) Parsons Tunnel the railway hugs the cliff face and runs adjacent to the Teignmouth Sea Wall to Teignmouth station. The line was opened on 30 May 1846 by the South Devon Railway.

As the railway approaches the town of Teignmouth, the line veers away from the sea. Originally the route went into Eastcliffe Tunnel on the approach to the station, but this was opened out in 1884 to allow for station expansion and the doubling of the track. Between opening and 1884 a 'loop' was provided on the Teignmouth Sea Wall section to increase line capacity. A tunnel also existed at the west end of Teignmouth station but this was removed in 1881

opposite Sea Lawn Terrace, Dawlish, where it dropped to virtually beach height; it was built in this way as the affluent residents and land owners of Sea Lawn House and Sea Lawn Terrace did not want the 'peasants' walking the wall to be able to gawp into their property. After the dreadful storms on 5 and 14 February 2014 a major rethink of the integrity of the sea wall took place, and to ensure the long-term security of the rail line, the wall and the preservation of the adjacent properties it was agreed to raise the lower section of the wall to full height. This met some objections from local property owners but this was overcome and a new full height wall section was built in late 2014 early 2015, allowing for the first time a flat walkway all the way between Dawlish and Dawlish Warren.

The original single line railway between Dawlish Warren and Dawlish was doubled in May 1858 to meet traffic demands. Broad gauge track gave way to standard gauge lines from 22 May 1892.

The original Dawlish station was opened in 1846, on the same site as the present structure; it was built of wood and iron, and had an overall train shed, but this was sadly burnt down on 14 August 1873. The present brick and stone built structure was opened on 12 April 1875. Over the years many alterations have been made, the original steel glazed roof gave way to a concrete and perspex structure in 1961 and was further replaced in the spring of 2014. The original footbridge fell into a poor state in the early years of this century and in 2012 was replaced with a plastic-over-steel-frame bridge, formed to a period design to fit in with the station. This bridge provides the only link between the 'up' and 'down' side of the station. Today few passenger facilities exist; the booking office on the lower level is still open and during the day the station platforms are manned. To provide disabled access to the down side a light-controlled staff-assisted foot crossing exists at the country end of the station. With today's safety-led railway, this archaic feature should be replaced with proper disabled access to the 'down' side. The station received some damage during the 2014 storms and much remedial work was carried out, improving the passenger environment, including the provision of flower tubs.

Returning to the sea wall itself, roughly mid-way between Dawlish Warren and Dawlish a bridge known as Black Bridge or Rockstone Bridge links the Exeter Road with the sea wall and beach. This was originally a concrete structure, replaced with a more modern wooden deck in the 1980s. Further towards Dawlish a metal single-width private footbridge existed until the early 1970s linking Sea Lawn Terrace and the sea wall.

A Coastguards' lookout together with a boathouse below at the water line was erected in 1846, just to the London end of Dawlish station. This was originally manned by HM Preventative Services and later the Coastguard service. The Coastguard station closed during town development work.

At the same time Eastcliffe Tunnel was removed, and the iconic and picturesque 'Skew Bridge' which dominates photographs taken at the east end of Teignmouth was erected.

Teignmouth station was originally the terminus of the line from Exeter, becoming a through station when the line was extended to Newton Abbot from 17 December 1847. Originally it was operated by the atmospheric system, but by September of 1848 this had been abandoned and normal loco-hauled operation introduced.

For the first two years of life, Teignmouth station had just a single platform, but soon traffic levels demanded additional facilities.

In keeping with the rest of the sea wall route, broad gauge track was replaced with standard gauge on 20 May 1892 and between then and 1895 the station was totally rebuilt, with an opulent, large structure, much in keeping with other major West Country holiday towns such as Weston-super-Mare and Torquay. At Teignmouth the station facilities were built on the 'down' side. Much of the station building remains today, although largely modified from its original use. Such was the growth of passenger traffic using Teignmouth, with a huge number of holiday trains serving the station, that by 1938 the 'down' platform was extended to accommodate up to 15-coach trains.

Teignmouth had a small goods yard, located on the 'up' side with a very tight entrance at the Exeter end of the 'up' platform. General freight traffic was handled by the station until 14 June 1965 and coal traffic until the end of 1967 when all facilities were closed. Today the former goods yard is the site of industrial units.

Signalling at Teignmouth was controlled by a small manual signal box with 31 levers, located at the west end of the 'down' platform, opened in 1896 to replace an original structure. Teignmouth signal box was closed on 15 November 1986 as part of the West of England modernisation with control passing to Exeter Panel Box.

After departing from Teignmouth, trains pass through a brick and stone face cutting, through a largely residential area until Teignmouth Docks are reached, operated today by Associated British Ports (ABP). The port was rail connected until 1969 and had its own signal box - Teignmouth Old Quay. Access into Teignmouth Docks was a difficult operation with too tight an access from the 'down' line, thus all movements to and from the docks were from the 'up' line, crossing over the 'down' track.

Directly to the west end of Teignmouth station is a facing crossing from the 'up' to 'down' line; this is a signalled crossover for trains heading west using the bi-directional 'up' track from Dawlish Warren. When installed during the west of England resignalling it was designed for use during periods of inclement weather. However, with an increased number of trains now using the route, bi-directional running can now be instigated without special instructions and is frequently used if trains are running out of schedule; usually stopping trains are operated on the bi-directional track, allowing fast trains to keep to the main track, but is no way the rule.

After passing Teignmouth Docks, the line now skirts the River Teign and heads towards Shaldon Bridge, a structure which allows excellent photographs of the line. From Shaldon Bridge the line continues to follow the River Teign towards Bishopsteignton and Newton (the suffix Abbot was not added until 1877); this section was opened on 30 December 1846 with the extension of the line from Teignmouth.

Heading west, the line passes close to the village of Bishopsteignton, which has never had a station, before arriving at Newton Abbot, on the way passing Hackney yard, Newton Abbot race course and the site of the huge depot and workshops of the Great Western Railway and BR on the 'down' side.

Just before Newton Abbot station was the junction with the Moretonhampstead line. This branch closed to passengers in February 1959, and goods traffic was cut back to Bovey from April 1964, being further truncated to Heathfield in July 1970. The line is

Below: While the majority of CrossCountry Trains are formed of Class 220 and 221 'Voyager' stock, four HST sets are operated by the company and operate on the more heavily loaded services. Based at Edinburgh Craigentinny, these sets normally operate three diagrams on weekdays and four on Saturdays. On 6 August 2014, Class 43 No. 43357 passes Dawlish with train 1V44, the 06.00 Leeds to Paignton Summer Saturday service. **CJM**

now operated as a freight-only spur to Teigngrace and Heathfield. After seeing limited freight traffic over the last quarter of the 20th century, the Heathfield line saw a new traffic flow from woodlands of Devon and Cornwall when Colas Rail Freight commenced the operation of log trains between Teigngrace and the Kronospan sidings at Chirk in North Wales in December 2011. The logs were harvested from controlled sites in Devon and Cornwall and taken by road to Teigngrace for loading. This was a difficult operation in terms of both road and rail operations and from mid-2015 the traffic was transferred to spare capacity in Exeter Riverside Yard.

At Newton Abbot, the original South Devon Railway station was in need of replacement in the immediate pre-First World War years, and plans were drawn up to build a much larger structure in a revised location. The original goods depot was moved to new premises on the Moretonhampstead line, while sidings were laid on Hackney Marshes opening towards the end of 1911.

After World War I, the new Newton Abbot station was constructed, now facing the town and on to Queen Street. The new station was formally opened on 11 April 1927.

Adjacent to the station was Newton Abbot works and locomotive and stock depot. The works was used extensively in the late 1800s to rebuild broad gauge stock to standard gauge and played an important role in rolling stock operations right up until the mid-1970s. The workshops, with a traverser, were responsible for heavy maintenance on diesel-hydraulic classes, while a significant carriage works existed at the west end of the site. Sidings were located between the depot and station; in later years these were supplemented by a carriage washing plant.

In modern traction days a diesel depot and carriage depot existed, together with fuelling and service points.

The diesel depot closed in the mid-1970s and the site fell into disrepair, being largely demolished in the 1990s with some of the original buildings and new structures now used as industrial units.

The yard at Hackney has seen intermittent use over the years. When Stoneycombe Quarry was open the sidings were used for ballast train stabling, while in the early years of this century Freightliner Heavy Haul used the sidings for recessing the Moorswater cement trains, and ballast services operating from Cornwall. From 2014, Colas Rail Freight and Freightliner Heavy Haul used the sidings to drop off rail for reprocessing, an operation which appeared to have ended in 2015.

Newton Abbot, with its many lines, junctions and connections, had two large signal boxes from 1926/27 until West of England resignalling in 1987. Newton Abbot East box had a staggering 206 levers while Newton Abbot West boasted 153 levers.

On the subject of signalling, an intermediate box on the Teignmouth to Newton Abbot section existed at Bishopsteignton until 1969 and another at Hackney operated between 1891 and 1971.

In terms of photography, the line between Shaldon Bridge and Newton Abbot is the least accessible. A private bridge crosses the line at Teignmouth boat yard but fencing now restricts photography. A way under the line near to Bishopsteignton and a small footpath overbridge allow limited access. A couple of private overbridges exist adjacent to campsites along the River Teign towards Newton Abbot. The shores of the river around Hackney Marshes can be accessed from a drive way to The Passage House Inn, with limited views of down trains possible. Photography at Newton Abbot station is good and a road overbridge at the west end of the station gives a good vantage point looking towards the station.

Until the late 1980s, west of Newton Abbot was Aller Junction, the point at which trains to Torquay, Paignton and Kingswear diverged off the main line towards Totnes, Plymouth and Cornwall.

At the opening of the railway, two single tracks were laid west from Newton Abbot and after one mile veered away from each other. The first physical junction brought into use on 29 January 1855 was Torquay Junction, which came about as the two tracks west of Newton Abbot now both serviced the Plymouth line with a single-line spur to the Paignton and Kingswear route.

From 1874 a third track was laid from the junction to Newton Abbot station, which was used by Paignton and Kingswear line services. Growth in traffic was such that a fourth track between Newton Abbot and Torquay Junction opened as part of the doubling of the Newton Abbot to Kingskerswell section of the line.

At the time of the original plans to rebuild Newton Abbot station prior to World War I it was proposed to build a flying junction by the village of Aller, close to Torquay Junction, which would allow high speed divergence and joining of trains from both lines. However, the outbreak of hostilities saw this plan shelved and on 25 May 1925 a new junction was installed at Aller, known as Aller Junction. The layout of the tracks was complex and pairs of lines were grouped by direction. From right to left when looking at the layout west from Aller it was 'down' Paignton, 'down' Plymouth, 'up' Paignton and 'up' Plymouth. The junction layout at Aller allowed full interconnection between lines.

This arrangement was not welcomed by operators, for it required all 'up' Paignton line trains to cross over the 'down' Plymouth line, which caused serious delays at times of peak traffic, especially on Summer Saturdays.

However, the arrangement remained until the West of England resignalling which called for a simpler layout. Just three tracks were provided west from Newton Abbot for around half a mile, where the Paignton route split into two tracks. The two twin-track routes then ran side by side to the point of the former Aller Junction before diverging to their respective destinations. At this time, April 1987, Aller Junction was officially renamed Aller Divergence and the lines at the junction from right to left looking west were renamed 'down' Paignton, 'up' Paignton, 'down' Plymouth and 'up' Plymouth. ■

Below: *West Coast Railway Co Class 37 No. 37685 passes Cockwood Harbour on 18 September 2010 powering train 1Z57 the 09.20 Solihull to Plymouth, transferrying stock to the Plymouth area for a steam charter.* **CJM**

Recorded from the footpath on Lea Mount, high above Dawlish and giving a view right along the sea wall to Dawlish Warren, the Great Western Railway-liveried HST set, formed of power cars Nos. 43188 and 43187 with passenger set No. LA15, form train 1C84, the 14.06 Paddington to Penzance on 12 October 2015. **CJM**

Around the Exeter area

Above: To the east of Exeter lays Cowley Bridge, the junction for the Taunton and Crediton lines. A mechanical signal box existed here until 1985 when the route was resignalled and control passed to Exeter Panel Signal Box. The original box was erected in 1894 to replace a Bristol & Exeter Railway cabin. Originally the box was only two-thirds its later length, being extended in 1943 when goods lines were lengthened in the area. The box nameboard was after this time not centrally placed. Originally the box had 16 levers, but this was extended to 19 in 1916 and 20 by 1924. Major work in 1942 saw a 35-lever frame installed only to be extended a year later to a 44-lever frame. This view of the box was recorded in summer 1980. **CJM**

Left Upper: For several years in the early part of this century, Network Rail recommenced the operation of loaded ballast trains from Meldon Quarry, which was first opened by the L&SWR in 1897. These trains were normally operated by Freightliner Heavy Haul feeding various virtual quarry sites. On 8 June 2005, No. 66526 passes the site of the original Cowley Bridge Junction signal box with the 10.30 Meldon Quarry to Oxford Hinksey yard. **CJM**

Left Lower: Dominating the background of many pictures taken at Cowley Bridge Junction is the Cowley Bridge Inn, now known as the New Inn after a take-over in early 2015. The building was a public house until 2008 when it became a Chinese restaurant which closed after serious flooding. On 13 April 2005, Virgin Trains 'Super Voyager' No. 221111 passes the Cowley Bridge Inn forming the 10.05 Glasgow Central to Penzance service. **CJM**

Above: *With Exeter Middle Box behind, Class 25 No. 25223 pulls into Exeter St Davids on 28 June 1976 with the 07.35 mixed passenger/van service from Barnstaple. After the diesel-hydraulic classes were withdrawn, Classes 25 and 31 became common on Exeter local services.* **CJM**

Below: *Taken on 6 April 2015, this is the present-day view from the Taunton end of Exeter St Davids. The GW box has gone, colour light signals prevail, but the general track layout remains the same. A FGW HST, led by advertising-liveried No. 43144, approaches the station with train 1C73, the 09.04 Taunton to Penzance.* **CJM**

Above: *Although largely modernised, much of the original 1864 station facade remains at Exeter St Davids. Several retail units now exist and the road outside restructured to take bus and road traffic as well as car parking and taxi facilities.* **CJM**

Left: *Exeter Panel Signal Box, built as part of the 1985 West of England resignalling project, is located at the west of the station adjacent to the multiple unit depot. In recent years steel fencing has been erected around the structure to reduce unwanted visitors. This view shows the box in its 2015 condition.* **CJM**

Below: *In recent years the depot facility adjacent to Exeter St Davids station has been expanded and modernised to maintain second generation DMU vehicles. One of the depot's Class 150/1 sets No. 150130 is seen stabled by modern fuel and servicing equipment; further upgrading and expansion of the depot is planned, with newer units soon to be allocated to Exeter.* **CJM**

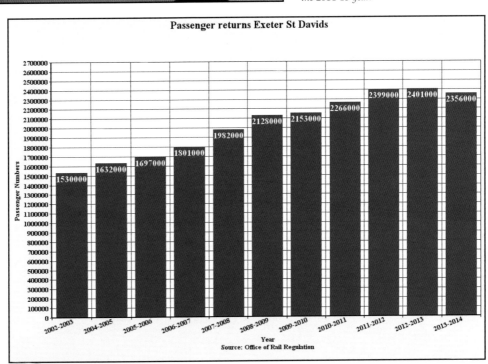

Below: *Exeter St Davids passenger returns for the period 2002-2014, showing in the main a steady increase in passenger numbers, rising over 800,000 in ten years. The reduction in passenger numbers for 2013-14 was due to the Dawlish Sea Wall collapse and the fact there were no through trains for eight weeks, which saw a huge reduction in through journeys. The ORR reports a further positive increase to date in the 2014-15 year.*

Top: *Exeter DMU servicing depot by night, showing the recently built three-vehicle fuel and exam facility.* **CJM**

Above: *21 August 2014 was a very important day for Exeter, when First Great Western hosted the RAF Red Arrows aerobatic display team and invited the squadron to re-name Class 43 power car No. 43155 in their honour. The suggestion to re-apply the Red Arrows name to No. 43155, which carried the name in its Virgin Trains days, was put forward by Dawlish Air Show organiser and train driver Kevin Wills. Each year the Red Arrows perform one of their stunning displays at the Dawlish Air Show and the chance was taken to say a special thank you to the RAF team to mark their 50th season of public displays. The entire 2014 aerobatic squadron poses by the newly named power car with First Great Western Exeter Manager David Crome. The Red Arrows power car was used two days later on a special Exeter to Newton Abbot shuttle service during the 2014 Dawlish Air Show.* **CJM**

Passenger returns Exeter St Davids

Year	Passenger Numbers
2002-2003	1530000
2004-2005	1632000
2005-2006	1697000
2006-2007	1801000
2007-2008	1982000
2008-2009	2128000
2009-2010	2153000
2010-2011	2266000
2011-2012	2399000
2012-2013	2401000
2013-2014	2356000

Source: Office of Rail Regulation

Above: *Exeter St Davids is a complex station, having directly at its west end the connection with Exeter Central and the ex-L&SWR route to London via Yeovil. This route today sees a lot of traffic with in addition to Waterloo services, trains working on a half-hourly basis to and from Exmouth. Trains on the main line are still permitted to arrive and depart from any of the six through platforms with junction facilities at both ends of the station. FGW's mock-Great Western-liveried Class 57 No. 57604 arrives in Exeter St Davids platform 1 on 26 July 2014 with a service from Par, having crossed over from the 'up' main on crossings by the River Exe bridge. A light-controlled barrow crossing still exists at the west end of the station but is seldom used.* **CJM**

Left Middle: *The South West Trains services to/from Waterloo are formed of Class 159 stock and operate on an hourly basis. Services from Exeter Central are only able to gain access to platforms 1 and 3. On 6 April 2015, Class 159s Nos. 159108 and 159007 arrive at Exeter St Davids platform 3 with train 1L09, the 07.45 service from Salisbury. After discharging its passengers, the set will work forward into Exeter West Yard to change direction and return to platform 1 for a departing service to Waterloo.* **CJM**

Left Bottom: *In the mid-1970s, following the demise of smaller diesel-hydraulic locos from Devon branch line services, principally on the Exeter to Barnstaple and Paignton lines, Class 25 and 31 locos were drafted in. On 13 July 1976, Class 31/1 No. 31112 arrives at Exeter St Davids from the west and passes the water tower where the present Exeter Panel Signal Box is located, with a Newton Abbot to Exeter stopping service.* **Brian Morrison**

Above: *Today, Class 143, 150 and 153 stock shares local branch line duties. Class 143 Nos. 143619 and 143618 depart from Exeter St Davids on 17 June 2014 with the 13.43 Barnstaple to Exmouth service.* **CJM**

Right: *CrossCountry 'Voyager' No. 220020 departs from Exeter St Davids platform 4, with the 06.10 Derby to Plymouth on 6 April 2015.* **CJM**

Below: *Class 25 No. 25220 departs from Exeter St Davids and crosses the River Exe bridge on 3 July 1976 with the 17.10 Exeter to Laira empty stock service.* **Bernard Mills**

Left: *Originally built by the South Devon Railway in 1846, the station of Exeter St Thomas was closer to the city and docks than the main station. It is built on a 501 yard (458m) stone viaduct. Between September 1846 and September 1847 it served the atmospheric system. Built as a single line, the second track was added in 1861. Originally having an overall roof, this was demolished in the 1960s and the station is now unstaffed and a halt with high stairs to reach the platforms on both sides and no disabled access. Here is the station in 2015.* **CJM**

Right: *Today, Exeter St Thomas is only serviced by the stopping services from Exmouth/Exeter to Paignton, except for one through service to/from London each day. Being on a viaduct, access to the station platforms is difficult and these three-flight steel stairs are the only entrance to the 'up' (Exeter-bound) platform.* **CJM**

≷ Exeter St Thomas
↖ Trains for Dawlish Warren, Dawlish, Teignmouth, Newton Abbot and beyond
Under the bridge for trains to Exeter St Davids

Exeter St Thomas

First Great Western

Exeter St Thomas

Left: *The original station buildings are on the 'down' (Newton Abbot-bound) side and today have been sold and currently operate as a food outlet. The public access to the westbound platform is steep stone steps at the east end of the building, which are a frequent hang-out for drunks and drug addicts, rendering the station somewhat unwelcoming, especially in the evening. The station entrance on the 'down' side is seen in mid-April 2015.* **CJM**

Above: *Apart from the stopping services on the Exeter-Paignton corridor, which operate approximately hourly, Exeter St Thomas sees all through services between Exeter and Newton Abbot. Viewed from the 'down' platform, a Network Rail test train comprising Class 31 No. 31105, with vehicles 6264, 977983 and DBSO 9703, forms train 3Z33, the 14.00 Laira to Derby Railway Technical Centre, on 19 September 2014.*
CJM

Right Middle: *On 27 November 2011 First Great Western said farewell to the Class 142s, with the remaining sets being transferred to Northern Rail, and replaced by Class 150/1 sets. To mark the end of the design working off Exeter depot a railtour was organised, the 'Pacer Finale', which visited several of the Devon branches as well as Alphington Road (the remaining stump of the Teign Valley line) and Heathfield. Sets Nos. 142001, 142063 and 142068 approach Exeter St Thomas on the 'down' line, before crossing over to gain entry into Alphington Road.*
Antony Christie

Right Below: *The Office of Rail Regulation passenger returns for Exeter St Thomas show a massive increase over this 11-year period increasing by some 150,000 annual journeys. This increase is due to major retail development in the lower part of Exeter City the regeneration of the Exeter Quay area and more people using this station to feed the city centre. Like other stations on the route the closure of the sea wall for eight weeks at the start of 2014 impacted on passenger figures, with a loss of around 9,000 journeys.*

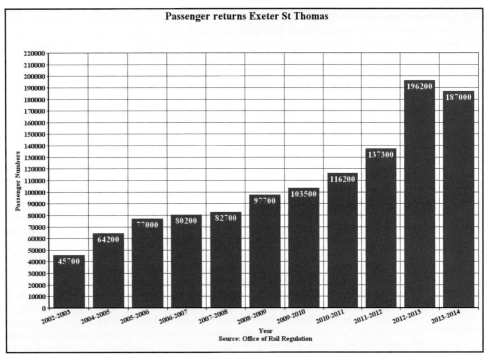

Passenger returns Exeter St Thomas

Above: *The small stub of the former Teign Valley line at Alphington Road is now operated as a private siding feeding the Exeter branch of Sims Metal Management. The line, fed off the 'up' main line just west of Exeter St Thomas, sees infrequent scrap metals trains running loaded to Cardiff. Today the trains are operated by DB-Schenker, but for a period in 2012-2013 GBRf operated the service. On 13 March 2013, Class 66 No. 66711 shunts a rake of high-capacity box wagons into the siding. The steep grade on the right once served Exeter City Basin yard.* **Antony Christie**

Below: *From time to time enthusiast tours request to traverse the remaining stub of the Teign Valley line, returning passenger traffic to the long-closed route. On 17 April 2010 UK Railtours operated 'The Dartmoor Railway & Okehampton' charter, which ran from Paddington to Alphington Road headed by Class 66 No. 66182, before working to Okehampton powered by No. 66002. The train is seen descending from the connection with the Great Western main line and heading into the Marsh Barton industrial complex.* **Antony Christie**

Left: *From the earliest days of UK railways Royal Mail traffic, both letters and parcels, was shipped by train. However, post-privatisation and under the remit of EWS, the Royal Mail contract ended after EWS and Royal Mail could not strike a financial deal to continue operation of the service. In early 2004 the last 'Mail by Rail' services operated. In terms of the Exeter to Newton Abbot line a number of mail and Travelling Post Office trains operated. Powered by a pair of Rail Express Systems Class 47s, Nos. 47567 Red Star and 47780 pass Matford on 23 June 1994 forming the 16.45 Plymouth to Newcastle mail service.* **CJM**

Above: *After the twin-track railway heads west through Exeter St Thomas and Marsh Barton, it proceeds towards Exminster and the banks of the River Exe. With the city skyline of Exeter in the background including the Cathedral on the right and the industrial complex of Marsh Barton at the rear of the train, Colas Rail Freight Class 56 No. 56094 heads west on 19 September 2012 with empty log wagons from wood processor Kronospan in Chirk to Teigngrace for loading.* **Antony Christie**

Below: *Carrying Waterman Railways lined black livery, based on that of the London & North Western Railway, Class 47/7 No. 47710* Lady Godiva *pilots Rail Express Systems No. 47761 towards Gissons bridge, Exminster, on 8 August 1994 forming the afternoon Plymouth to Newcastle vans. In the far distance behind the train the road bridge over the long-closed Exminster station can be seen.* **CJM**

Britain's Scenic Railways Dawlish - The Railway from Exeter to Newton Abbot

Powderham to Starcross

Above: *West from Exminster the twin-track line continues over Exminster marshes and soon hugs the bank of the River Exe and heads towards the grounds of the Powderham Estate, the home of the Earl of Devon since the 1300s. Since the railway opened, a footpath has existed from close to Powderham Church towards Exeter along the bank of the river. In 2014 a new bridge was erected over the line and the user-operated gate crossing closed. The bridge, officially part of the Exe estuary cycle route, cost £1.6million and links Powderham with Turf Lock. The bridge has provided a new and very good photographic viewpoint. This is the afternoon view looking back towards Exeter and shows the River Exe on the right, with the village of Topsham in the middle distance. Taken on 24 March 2015, the 06.06 Edinburgh Waverley to Plymouth CrossCountry service is formed with power cars Nos. 43378 and 43366.* **CJM**

Left Middle: *The 3m-wide Powderham footbridge was built by locally based contractor Dawnus Construction and has ramped access on both sides with a single-span deck crossing the railway. The structure has been built with a height envelope that would allow electrification at a future date (highly unlikely). This is the view from the Powderham Church side looking towards Exeter. The five-bar gate on the right is an emergency access and normally kept locked.* **CJM**

Left Below: *The late-afternoon sun at Powderham crossing or bridge is almost perfect for any Exeter-bound train. On 22 July 2012, BR Standard No. 70000 Britannia heads east with the 16.50 Kingswear to Bristol Temple Meads 'Torbay Express' service.* **CJM**

Above: *Network Rail carried out an inspection of the rail route from Reading to Paignton via Bristol and return by way of the Berks & Hants route on 27 May 2015. The train was formed of inspection saloon No. 975025* Caroline, *an original Hastings line buffet car which for many years was the Southern Region General Manager's saloon and hit world news when on 29 July 1981 it was used to carry Charles, Prince of Wales and his new wife Diana on the first leg of their honeymoon from London Waterloo to Romsey. Powered by DRS Class 37/4 No. 37402, No. 975025 is seen approaching Powderham bridge forming the 14.47 Paignton to Reading.* **CJM**

Below: *Due to planned maintenance of the usual New Measurement Train (NMT), a stand-in formation of vehicles 977997 and 5981 was made up with Class 67s Nos. 67018* Keith Heller *and 67012* A Shropshire Lad *working 'top and tail'. On 17 April 2015 the formation operated test train 1Q18, the 05.07 Old Oak Common to Paddington via Plymouth, seen approaching Powderham from the new bridge on its outbound journey.* **Antony Christie**

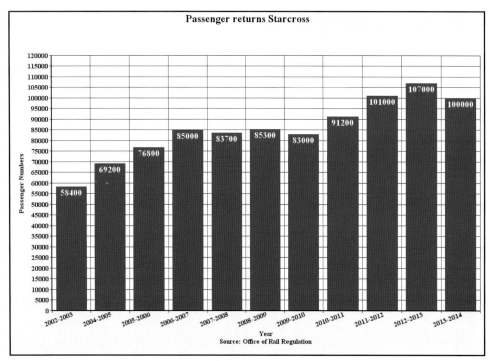

Passenger returns Starcross

Source: Office of Rail Regulation

First Great Western

Top: *West of Powderham the railway, still skirting the River Exe, passes through Starcross, a small village which still has an operational station served by Exeter-Paignton services. On 8 September 1989 Class 47/0 No. 47217 pilots Class 50 No. 50015 Valiant towards Starcross forming the previous day's 15.00 Coatbridge to Tavistock Junction air brake freight. The Class 50 was being transported dead in the train and was en route to Laira depot for attention.* **CJM**

Left Middle: *At the west end of Starcross station are the remains of the original atmospheric pumping house, complete with a truncated tower, which is now the home of the Starcross Fishing and Cruising Club. On 23 March 2015, 'Voyager' No. 220007 hurries through Starcross station with the 10.07 Paignton to Manchester Piccadilly service. Starcross station provides the access for the summer Exmouth ferry service, which is located on a pier from the west end of the 'down' platform.* **CJM**

Left Bottom: *As can be seen from the table, Starcross is another station which has good passenger growth over the past 11 years, with some slight reductions in both 2007-08 and 2009-10. Again the drop in passenger numbers in the 2013-14 year is attributable to the line closure for eight weeks.*

Starcross
Alight here for Exmouth Ferry

Above: *Platform facilities at Starcross are sparse to say the least, with limited waiting shelters. Neither platform provides disabled access, and at a station such as this it might be hard to provide when the legal requirement comes into force in 2020. Viewed from the station footbridge on 23 March 2015, the 10.00 Cardiff to Paignton service passes through non-stop formed of Class 153 set No. 153333, painted in FGW-branded London Midland livery, and Class 158 No. 158766.* **CJM**

Right Middle & Right Lower: *The upper view is looking west from the 'up' eastbound platform at Starcross, while the view below is taken from the westbound 'down' platform and is looking east towards Powderham and Exeter. Both:* **CJM**

Cockwood and the Exe Estuary

Above: *One of the most popular locations to capture railway images is Cockwood Harbour. On 9 September 1979, Class 33 No. 33005 powers eight Mk1 and Mk2 vehicles forming the 17.10 Newton Abbot to Exeter St Davids, complete with a buffet car. A far cry from today's Class 143 service on this route.* **Bernard Mills**

Left: *It is possible to capture good pictures of trains approaching Cockwood from the east, especially in the low evening light. On 6 January 2015 FGW Class 57/6 No. 57602 is seen coupled on the rear of the 14.00 Laira to Old Oak Common empty sleeper stock.* **CJM**

Below: *On 10 June 2000, when Virgin Trains was still using loco-hauled stock on many of its CrossCountry services, some Summer Saturday services were formed of West Coast Mk3 stock with a DVT. In this view, green-liveried Class 47 No. 47488 leads a Mk3 DVT and set over Cockwood Harbour with an afternoon Paignton to Manchester Piccadilly service.* **CJM**

Above: *It is possible with care to climb the hills to the west side of Cockwood Harbour and obtain images of westbound trains approaching the causeway. On 30 May 2015, Colas Rail Freight Class 66 No. 66846 approaches the harbour with train 6Z50, the 08.13 Chirk to Teigngrace empty log train.* **CJM**

Right: *With water in the harbour, which always improves the picture, Class 67 No. 67014 heads east on 1 July 2000 with the return of 'The Spanish Inquisition' railtour from Carne Point (Fowey) to Finsbury Park, formed of an immaculate green-liveried Mk1 rake.* **CJM**

Below: *The Exeter to Newton Abbot line has been strongly associated with the Colas Class 70s ever since they were introduced in early 2014, bringing a little colour to the coast. On 16 May 2015, No. 70803 crosses Cockwood Harbour with train 6C21, the 17.47 Westbury to Truro via Penzance, formed of ballast and SB Rail Kirow crane No. DRK 81624.* **CJM**

Dawlish Warren and Langstone Rock

Above: *The world-famous Dawlish Sea Wall commences when trains turn away from skirting the River Exe at Dawlish Warren and start to hug the coastline through Dawlish and on to Teignmouth. Some excellent views can be gained from around Langstone Rock, where this view of Class 50 No. 50046* Ajax *was taken powering the 10.55 Exeter St Davids to Paignton on 7 September 1989.* **CJM**

Below: *Looking west from the 'up' platform at Dawlish Warren in the summer of 1953, Great Western 'Hall' 4-6-0 No. 5999* Wollaton Hall *passes through on the middle road with an express parcels, while a westbound freight awaits the signal from the 'down' loop track. Since this image was recorded the 'up' platform at Dawlish Warren had been considerably shortened.* **E. D. Bruton**

Above: *Dawlish Warren signal box was located at the Exeter end of the 'down' platform it was opened for use on 12 October 1911 and was of GWR Type 7D, housing 58 levers. It remained in use until being abolished as part of the West of England resignalling, closing in the early hours of 14 November 1986. Although closed it was not demolished until 1990.* **CJM**

Above Left: *It could not be described as welcoming in any way, but this is the main entrance to Dawlish Warren 'up' side platform. The station does have a very small semi-open waiting shelter and in 2014 was equipped with an electronic passenger information system.* **CJM**

Above Right: *For many years until the late 1990s this amazing wooden notice with cut-out wooden letters, mounted on two lengths of rail, was to be found on the sea wall at Dawlish Warren giving notice not to dig, excavate or remove any soil, shingle, gravel or stone between Dawlish Warren and Teignmouth for a distance of 30 yards from the railway. Another sign of the same type was erected on the sea wall at Teignmouth.* **CJM**

Right: *While passenger traffic at Dawlish Warren is obviously seasonal, a considerable number of daily travellers do use the station to travel to Exeter for work or school or westwards to Dawlish, Teignmouth and Torquay for the same purpose. In common with other stations growth has been considerable over the past 10-11 years, with around 90,000 more journeys in 2013 than in 2002. The drop in passengers in 2013-14 was due to the sea wall collapse and no trains for eight weeks between February and April.*

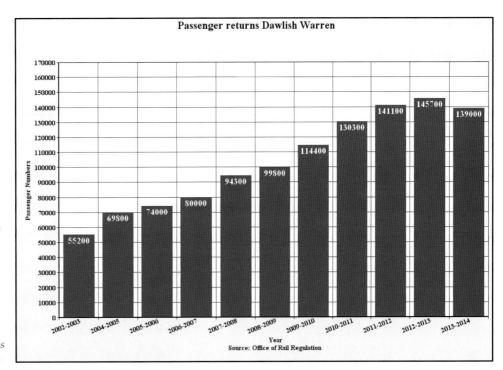

Passenger returns Dawlish Warren

Year	Passenger Numbers
2002-2003	55200
2004-2005	69800
2005-2006	74000
2006-2007	80000
2007-2008	94300
2008-2009	99800
2009-2010	114400
2010-2011	130300
2011-2012	141100
2012-2013	145700
2013-2014	139000

Source: Office of Rail Regulation

Above: *Just to the west of the present Dawlish Warren station is a footbridge which crosses the line, linking the car park with the sea wall. This was the site of the original Warren Halt, later Warren Platform, and was also the station footbridge, located at the Exeter end of the platforms. The footbridge actually pre-dates the platforms, being built in 1873. On 20 June 1981 the bridge provided the photographic platform for this view of Class 50 No. 50010* Monarch *powering the 07.50 Bristol Temple Meads to Penzance service. In the background the 1959 and 1981 camping coaches, then operated by the BR Staff Association, are seen.* **Bernard Mills**

Below: *Another view recorded from the Dawlish Warren footbridge, again looking towards Exeter, but this time from the 'up' side of the line. It was taken on 16 June 1981 and shows non-heat Class 47/3 No. 47334 heading west with a Stoke-on-Trent to Tavistock Junction air brake freight. Both the front and rear are formed of clay wagons returning to Cornwall for re-loading.* **CJM**

Above: *The very top of Langstone Rock offers a superb view around the entire area, but today the steps are a little treacherous and not for the faint-hearted. Class 52 'Western' No. D1040* Western Queen *traverses the sea wall towards Dawlish Warren on 5 January 1976 with the 09.20 relief service from Plymouth to Paddington.* **Bernard Mills**

Right: *In recent years the Red Rock Café has provided sustenance for walkers, bathers and railway photographers at the foot of Langstone Rock. A great meeting place for train followers.* **CJM**

Below: *On 29 May 2012, Freightliner Class 66/5 No. 66595 rounds the curve at Dawlish Warren and past the Red Rock Café with train 6Z27, the 08.21 Westbury Yard to Newton Abbot, Hackney Yard, formed of a loaded Network Rail 'Slinger' rail train.* **CJM**

Above: *The railways of Devon and Cornwall benefit from a very pro-active Devon & Cornwall Rail Partnership. Based at Plymouth University, the Partnership is a non-profit organisation, working to promote travel over the two counties' branch lines, which seeks methods of improvements to services and facilities and promotes the places served by the branch lines to help the local economy. The Partnership also supports engagement and two-way communication between the community and rail industry. In 2015 two Devon-based Class 153s were decorated in Partnership-based liveries as part of a promotion of local services supported by rail partnerships under the Citizensrail banner. No. 153325 in Citizensrail red livery departs from Dawlish Warren on 6 March 2015 with the 08.00 Cardiff to Paignton service.* **CJM**

Below: *Today, freight is very scarce on the sea wall section, with only two daily timetabled freight services each week that actually operate. However, additional and special trains do operate. In the days when the Moorswater cement worked, Freightliner Heavyhaul Class 66/6 No. 66619 rounds the curve at Dawlish Warren on 3 September 2010 with the afternoon Moorswater to Westbury, formed of 21 empty four-wheel PCA cement tanks. Since this image was recorded the car park on the right was turned into an engineering work site for the sea wall repair and rebuilding work.* **CJM**

Above: Images of trains rounding the curve at Dawlish Warren from the west are best obtained in the morning when the sun is on the sea side of the line. Many locations around the base of Langstone Rock exist. In 'Visit Plymouth' branding, FGW No. 43163 leads the 08.30 Penzance to Paddington on 13 July 2012. **CJM**

Below: Led by EWS Class 66/0 No. 66101, Pathfinder Tours charter train 1Z27, the 05.57 Whitchurch to Parkandillack 'The Duchy Explorer', heads onto the sea wall section at Dawlish Warren on 10 April 2010. The signal on the 'up' line allows for a signalled movement over the 'up' main, 'up' loop and to cross to the 'down' line. Additionally, a shunt signal is provided. **CJM**

The Dawlish Sea Wall

Britain's Scenic Railways Dawlish - The Railway from Exeter to Newton Abbot

Left Above: *Over the years, literally millions of pictures of trains must have been recorded from the iconic photographic spot of Rockstone or Black Bridge, located midway between Dawlish and Dawlish Warren. The views are excellent in both directions. Taken during the livery transition period after privatisation, the 06.45 Penzance to Paddington approaches Rockstone Bridge on 29 March 1997 led by Great Western-liveried No. 43190 with No. 43179 Pride of Laira on the rear, with a rake of InterCity-liveried stock.* **CJM**

Left Below: *Passing below Rockstone Bridge, Virgin Trains 'Super Voyager' No. 221110* James Cook *forms the 08.30 Penzance to Dundee service on 5 April 2007.* **CJM**

Top: *Little has changed if this and the image top left are compared. Recorded on 4 June 1949, 'Hall' 4-6-0 No. 4939* Littleton Hall *approaches Rockstone Bridge with the 10.00 Paignton to Cardiff service.* **E. D. Bruton**

Right Middle: *Dean Single, 3031 'Achilles' class No. 3027* Worcester *approaches Rockstone Bridge in the summer of 1912 with an 'up' passenger train formed of a varied collection of four-wheel and bogie stock.* **CJM-C**

Right Below: *By virtue of its location, the Dawlish Sea Wall seldom sees snow, and when it does it usually quickly melts away. On 17 February 1994 residents woke to find the town covered in white and in mid-morning this view of Class 150/2 No. 150278 was recorded from Rockstone Bridge forming a Paignton to Exeter service. In the distance a Class 158 can be seen heading west passing Sea Lawn Terrace.*
Nick Hewling

Above: *A stunning night image recorded from the deck of Rockstone Bridge looking west on 14 February 2009 shows EWS Class 66/0 No. 66117 parked on the 'up' line during track renewal work of the 'down' track between Sea Lawn Terrace and Dawlish station. To provide illumination for staff, temporary lighting had been erected which helps to illuminate the picture.* **Nathan Williamson**

Left Middle: *Viewed from the Rockstone Bridge looking east, towards Dawlish Warren, Langstone Rock dominates the backdrop. On 20 March 2015, a CrossCountry Trains Class 221 'Super Voyager' with its first class coach leading, heads west forming the 06.40 York to Plymouth service.* **CJM**

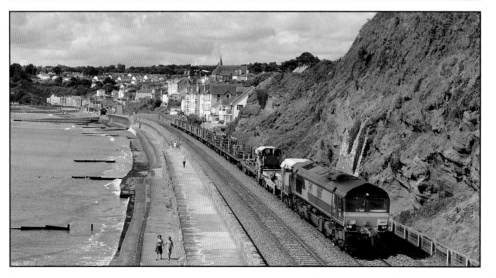

Left Below: *Engineering work west of Dawlish at weekends frequently sees works trains traverse the sea wall on a Sunday morning, returning trains to the West of England main engineering base at Westbury. On Sunday 11 July 2010, EWS Class 66/0 No. 66167 powers train 6W32, the 08.20 Totnes to Westbury, formed of a long welded rail train after an overnight rail drop near Rattery.* **CJM**

Above: *The sight and sound of a Class 52 'Western' traversing the sea wall stirs the hearts of many enthusiasts, and today, when the only preserved loco of the fleet with a main-line certificate powers trains over the route, hundreds of enthusiasts and photographers often turn out. On 10 May 2014, Vintage Trains 'Western Lickeys The Banks' tour, train 1Z52, the 07.00 Solihull to Plymouth, heads away from Rockstone Bridge towards Coastguards Bridge powered by maroon-liveried No. D1015* Western Champion. *The train is passing the containers used to protect the sea wall during rebuilding work following the February 2014 storms.* **CJM**

Right: *Approaching Coastguards Bridge, and passing the Dawlish outer home signal, blue-liveried 'Western' No. D1011* Western Thunderer *leads train 1C58, the 13.30 Paddington to Paignton, on 23 July 1969. At this time the crossover from the 'up' to 'down' line still existed below Coastguards Bridge.* **Bernard Mills**

Dawlish

The home of the black swans — First Great Western

Left Top & Left Middle: *The present Dawlish station was opened on 12 April 1875 to replace the original structure which was opened on 30 May 1846 and subsequently burnt down. The present buildings have been largely altered in more recent years with the original canopy replaced by a modern structure and a number of alterations made to the fabric of the building. The two views left show the 'up' platform from the Teignmouth and Dawlish Warren ends, as viewed from the 'down' platform. These show the 2015 condition of the structure. Both:* **CJM**

Left Bottom: *Dawlish has always been a busy station, with both local and holiday traffic, having annual growth almost doubling to 507,000 annual passenger numbers in 2012-13. The slightly reduced figure for 2013-14 due to the route closure is set to return to existing growth levels in the year 2014-15.*

Below: *A rather messy group of display and instruction boards is located to the left side of the main entrance to Dawlish station, which conveniently still houses a built-in Royal Mail collection box.* **CJM**

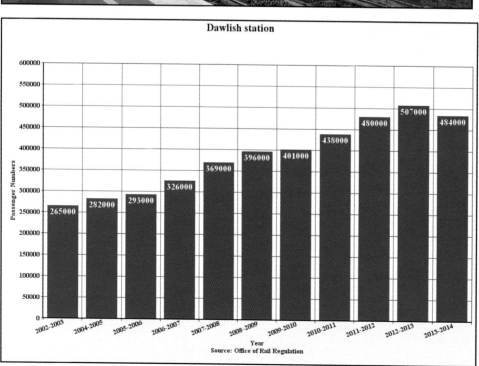

Dawlish station

Passenger Numbers / Year

Year	Passenger Numbers
2002-2003	265000
2004-2005	282000
2005-2006	293000
2006-2007	326000
2007-2008	369000
2008-2009	396000
2009-2010	401000
2010-2011	438000
2011-2012	480000
2012-2013	507000
2013-2014	484000

Source: Office of Rail Regulation

Right Top: *The main entrance to Dawlish station is located off Station Road, at the junction with Piermont Place (A379). The station is right on the sea front and the main station buildings which are still in use for both railway and retail purposes, are on the 'up' side. Entrance to the 'down' platform is by means of a footbridge; no access exists from the sea side. This is the view of the station entrance from Piermont Place in spring 2015.* **CJM**

Right Middle: *The vast majority of the 'down' platform at Dawlish is of wooden construction and overhangs the South Devon Coastal Path foot-way (sea wall), being supported by timber uprights. As can be seen from this illustration the structure is very open to the ingress of the sea during high winds and rough seas, and this is why the platform has frequently been blown or washed away.* **CJM**

Below: *With Dawlish signal box on the right still looking in quite good condition, but closed and devoid of its name-board, a CrossCountry HST set led by the final Class 43 power car No. 43198 approaches on 29 June 1996. The train is the 10.01 Summer Saturday service from Paignton to York.* **CJM**

DAWLISH
TO LET

LISTED SIGNAL BOX
SUITABLE FOR
OFFICE/STUDIO CONVERSION
AREA – APPROX. 200 sq.ft.

Please contact Jackie Curran on Tel.0272 348742

Property Board

DAWLISH SIGNAL BOX

Above Middle & Below: *The Great Western Railway Dawlish signal box was of unique design with just a 6ft wide base and with front and rear oversail. It was located on the 'up' platform and opened in January 1918. It remained in daily operation, fringing with Dawlish Warren and Teignmouth, until it was closed on 5 October 1986 as part of the West of England resignalling project. After closure the box was retained with the intention of letting out the structure for retail use. However, countless attempts at this have failed; even the author of this book inspected the structure with a view of taking it on as a shop. Sadly, the building fell into serious disrepair and by the mid-2000s had to be covered in plastic sheeting to avoid bits falling off onto passing trains or the public. Although listed,* this order was revoked in 2013 when permission was sought to demolish it. Notices were posted on 3 June 2013 that demolition was to take place with contractors working at night to remove the structure between 2 and 6 July 2013, returning the ground area to tarmac platform use. The view above shows the structure in the 1980s, while the view below was taken on 11 June 2013 and shows a Class 143 arriving on the 'down' line bound for Paignton. Both: **CJM**

Right: *The demolition notice, fixed to the box.* **CJM**

Above & Far Left: *The BR Property Board flyer to rent the box.* **CJM**

SITE NOTICE

PRIOR NOTIFICATION OF DEMOLITION

Town and Country Planning Act 1990 (as amended)
Town and Country Planning (General Permitted Development) Order 1995

An application to demolish the following building(s):

Location:	Dawlish Station, Station Road, Dawlish, EX7 9PJ
Description	Demolition of signal box
On or after:	17th June 2013

Has been submitted to Teignbridge District Council by:

Applicant/ Developer:	Network Rail
Date :	03.05.2013

The applicant has applied to the Local Planning Authority for a determination as to whether prior approval will be required for the method of demolition and any proposed restoration of the site.

The application details can be viewed on the Council's online planning register at
http://gis.teignbridge.gov.uk/TeignbridgePlanningOnline/Search.aspx or by visiting the Council's Offices at the address listed below.

If you wish to make any comments please send them in writing before:
(insert date 21 days after date of notice)

By e-mail to: planning@teignbridge.gov.uk

Or to: Planning Teignbridge District Council
Forde House
Brunel Road
Devon
TQ14 4XX

This Notice is to be displayed by the applicant / developer on or near the land on which the building to be demolished is sited and left in place for not less than 21 days in the period of 28 days beginning with the date on which the application is submitted to the local planning authority

Right: *Demolition of Dawlish signal box was undertaken by contractors working for Network Rail between 2 and 6 July 2013, working at night to avoid disruption to train services, or blocking the platform. Network Rail had to seek permission from Teignbridge Council to remove the structure, which was by now in a dangerous state and would soon become a risk to trains and the public. For several years the building was shored up by steel girders to avoid it falling over, while the brickwork was encased in thick plastic sheets to stop bits falling off. This was the view recorded on 4 July 2013, after the second night of demolition. On the first night the roof was removed and on the second the operating floor was taken away. All parts were loaded in road vehicles and disposed of locally.* **CJM**

Left: *By the morning of 5 July 2013, all that remained was the steel frame and the modern supporting structure. Overnight on 4/5 July the brick and plastic supports were removed and a clean-up of the ground area made. During demolition several spaces in the adjoining car park were closed to facilitate road vehicles and provide a stand for lighting.* **CJM**

Right: *By the morning of 8 July 2013 the site was cleared, the original steel frame for the structure remaining embedded in the platform. This was removed when the hole was filled and tarmac laid to bring the height of the platform to a uniform level. At the back, new steel fencing was installed and the car park spaces returned to use.* **CJM**

Dawlish – A Brief History

A settlement was first recognised to exist in Dawlish in 1044 when King Edward the Confessor granted the 'Parish of Dawlish' to his Chancellor and chaplain, Leofric, on condition that he built bridges and supplied soldiers to construct defences in time of war.

The charter explaining this donation is preserved at Exeter Cathedral. It is largely recorded in Latin and Anglo-Saxon English. While this is the oldest record of Dawlish in history, it is possible that a community existed well before, perhaps as far back as the 5th and 6th centuries AD, as the parish church of Dawlish is dedicated to St. Gregory the Great.

Under Leofric, the manor of Dawlish extended from roughly Teignmouth in the south to Cofton/Cockwood in the north, and to Haldon Hill in the west. This large area was mostly uninhabited and covered in forest, and would have been difficult to cultivate with poor soil.

The main reason settlers established a 'village' in the area was that it was protected, sheltered on three sides by hills and the remaining face by the sea. The presence of the sea provided limited food, while the wooded area harboured animals which gave meat, and wood for burning to give heating and a method of cooking, as well as for building. Freshwater rivers provided drinkable water. Work was provided by cultivating salt marshes which also gave a method of preserving food but above all gave trade with other communities.

At this time, what became known as Dawlish was not on the coast; the sea was feared, nobody knew what was 'over the water's edge', and it was known even in those days that damaging storms emerged from the sea which flooded the land, so they kept clear of the coastline.

The name Dawlish has developed over the years; the earliest recorded spelling is 'Doflisc' (Anglo-Saxon) or 'Dolfishe' (Latin). The exact meaning or derivation is unknown although it is considered to have meant 'a fruitful mead in a bottom, or on a river's side'.

Throughout the first century Dawlish was referred to by many names, but before it had been synonymous with 'Devil Water' and later 'Meadowland by Running Water', the latter being the motto adopted in the 20th century by the local council. Local history will tell that the name 'Devil Water', arose from the red waters which flow from the hills after heavy rain - this still happens today and it is quite frequent to find the stream running through the town bright red in colour after storms.

At the time Deawlisc (Dawlish) was a poor community, there was virtually no way of travel, and the only routes in or out would have been by rough cart tracks via Haldon. Early maps show one track towards Luscombe Hill and on towards the Teignmouth direction, one in the direction of Ashcombe towards Exeter, and a more substantial track between the port towns of Exeter and Teignmouth which also fed the expanding Dawlish community.

On Leofric's death in 1072, he gave his Manor and land of Dawlish to the Dean and Chapter of Exeter Cathedral. The area remained under Church control until 1807. After 1072, Dawlish is mentioned in the Doomsday Book, outlining the land and property owned by Bishop Osbern. It quotes that the bishop had

30 'villeins' (a person bound to the land and owned by the feudal lord), eight borders, three serfs, three cows, two swine, 100 sheep, a coppice three furlongs in length and one in breadth, six acres of meadowland and 12 acres of pasture. It was valued at just £8 a year.

The Doomsday entry shows that Dawlish had cultivated land with sheep as its main wealth. The villeins would have lived in cob-built houses, clustered around the church, and worked on the Bishop's land. They would have lived off beans, fruit and hard bread. Cider and ale would have been locally produced, providing a safer source of liquid than the water from the hills.

In 1080, the population is recorded at 400, and this grew only slowly; illness and disease were rife and this only improved with better food and water. Records show that the Black Death (Bubonic Plague) came to Dawlish in the 1340-50 period and almost annihilated the local population. Around this time some more wealthy gentry were starting to emerge, and these people were able to escape the effects of the plague as they seldom left their estates, not coming into contact with the sick working classes. The plague returned to Dawlish around 1629 for a few years.

The Industrial Revolution made significant changes to life in Dawlish, and the village quickly developed into a small town. The first industrial change was the opening of two flour mills, powered by water wheels, fed from the water course through the town. One, built in the late 1600s, was located in what is now Brunswick Place and the other, in around 1730, in Church Street. Another mill was located near Ashcombe.

By the end of the 18th century life in coastal towns such as Dawlish was starting to change, the fear of the sea had diminished and people started to extol the virtues of fresh sea air with possible healing qualities from the salty sea waters. Dawlish quickly found itself fashionable with the well-off or gentry. However, at the time travel was virtually impossible and the gentry were the only group who could afford to travel using a private coach. Few indications exist, but it is widely considered that Dawlish did not have a regular (if you could call it that) stagecoach until around 1812.

The new wealthy visitors to Dawlish changed the face of life in the area for ever; with transport so difficult, visitors usually arrived for long durations, often with extended families, complete with servants, typically for an entire summer season. In terms of town development this was fruitful, as many who enjoyed the area purchased land and later built property. The rough cob-built basic properties in Dawlish were not what the gentry sought and thus the area of residence grew, especially along the banks of the stream, known as the Brook. Soon a number of fine houses and villas were erected, using new and improved construction methods, allowing the previously unthought-of position for many properties adjacent to the sea. Indeed some early documentation actually refers to 'sea views' and bathing potential!

Sea bathing was recognised as a healthy and pleasurable pastime, but was very much a gentleman's 'hobby'. Ladies seem not to have been welcome to sea bathe until the latter part of the 19th century.

By 1803 Dawlish development was expanding, Dawlish resident John Manning masterminded improving the land either side of the Brook water course which ran down the middle of the town; this eventually allowed modern houses to be built closer to the seafront. His work straightened the course of the water in the town, with embankments built to reduce flooding. This work also led to the development of a new road, then known as Pleasant Row, now The Strand.

People often wonder why the two main roads of Dawlish, either side of the town, are so far apart, even with the relatively narrow water course between them. The reason is the problem of flooding, which although slightly controlled, has never gone away. Heavy rain on the hills to the back of the town builds up both capacity and speed as it rushes downhill towards the open sea. If there is a high tide, compounded by a south-west wind at the same time as high levels of water come from the hills, it has nowhere to go, and floods sideways onto the lower banks and flat lands either side in the lower part of the town.

One of the first reported incidents of major flooding causing damage was in 1810 when fast-flowing waters washed away eight bridges, much of the then newly created public lawns, embankments and two residential properties in what is now Brook Street. After this disaster, The Brook was further altered, with weirs built to prevent a recurrence. At this time, the grass area in the middle of the town, now known as 'The Lawn', was still grazed by sheep.

As Queen Victoria arrived on the throne, early plans were being made to bring the railway to Dawlish. A number of propositions were put forward in the 1830s, which led to the building and opening of Isambard Kingdom Brunel's Atmospheric Railway in 1846. The railway brought new life to the town.

One of the most momentous days in Dawlish history was Saturday 30 May 1846 when the first passenger train arrived; by today's standards it was slow, but the newspaper of the period hailed the train 'taking only 40 minutes to reach Dawlish from Exeter'. It is fascinating that the opening of the railway made Dawlish the first seaside resort to be served by rail west of Weston-super-Mare.

At the time, long-distance transport was very much the preserve of the upper classes. The majority of people worked six days a week and attended church twice on Sunday. Little time therefore existed to visit the seaside except at Public Holidays.

Development of Dawlish slowed at the end of the 19th century, but increased wealth for the town meant that living standards

Left Above: *Approaching Dawlish station and passing below the Coastguards footbridge, the 10.07 Bristol Temple Meads to Penzance is photographed from the 'down' platform on 6 April 2015 led by power car No. 43141.* **CJM**

Right: *During their first period of operating in the West Country, Class 142 'Skipper' set No. 142019 departs from Dawlish on 16 May 1986 forming the 09.33 Paignton to Exmouth service. By this time Dawlish box had closed and signalling controlled from Exeter Panel Signal Box.* **CJM**

improved, which saw the introduction of gas, an improved water supply, controlled sewerage, and even street lighting. Household electricity supplies were offered to those with sufficient funds.

Protection and safety of town folk was also improved, with a police officer being appointed in 1857. A Coastguard lookout was opened in 1868 to provide some protection for mariners; the building, now a private residence, still exists today.

In 1906 New Zealander John Nash introduced the now famous black swans to Dawlish. A Dawlish-born man, Nash emigrated during adulthood but paid frequent visits to the town and decided it needed some form of uniqueness. The black swans are still to be found on Dawlish Water, but today are supplemented by dozens of other non-native species.

In the early 1900s, workers from bigger industry and staff of the gentry began to receive paid holidays. This started the trend for holidays away from home, and saw a major upturn in visitor numbers to Dawlish, with some deciding after a couple of visits to purchase or build property in the area. These increases in numbers saw some 'smaller' housing (large by today's standards) built in streets such as Luscombe Terrace and Hatcher Street to the rear of the town, while open spaces in other roads were built over with quality housing. World War I stopped most further building until the early 1920s.

After the First World War, Dawlish became more established for the day trip market. This had an adverse effect on town life, which became less gentrified and more suited to the lower classes. The one and two week annual paid holiday became the norm and more people wanted to travel to seaside towns, mainly by train as motoring had yet to become the norm. At around the same time, wealthy folk from industrial areas, especially London, Birmingham and Liverpool, started to visit or retire to the area, leading to the once elegant villas being turned into hotels and guest houses.

The area east of Dawlish, which became known as Dawlish Warren, owes its success to the Great Western Railway which first built a station known as Warren Halt, close to Langstone Rock in 1905. Prior to this, only a few large houses and mansions were found on the hill behind the Warren. By 1929, with the introduction of air travel, Dawlish even had its own airport! The Great Western Railway built a small aerodrome on Haldon Hill, to serve the greater Torbay area on a Cardiff to Plymouth route. The Second World War sadly saw an end to the service. However, the airport remained in use for many years under military control, and remnants of the old airfield can still be identified today.

By the 1930s Dawlish had become popular as a low-budget resort, with an increasing number of holiday camps and caravan sites opening. The railway played a major role in this development, bringing thousands of people to the area every summer, with through running from most corners of the UK.

The outbreak of world hostilities again in 1939 brought further town development to a halt and considerably reduced holiday travel. The Second World War also ended a proposed plan which could have seen the railway disappear as we know it from the Dawlish seafront, with a scheme put forward by the Great Western Railway to build a Dawlish 'cut-off' line from Powderham via Gatehouse and Weech Road, seeing Dawlish served by a branch line.

In the year of Queen Elizabeth II's Coronation - 1953 - the Dawlish Town Council re-adopted the Latin phrase 'Pratum Juxta Rivos Aquarum' as its motto, which literally translates as 'Meadowland by Running Waters'. The heraldic emblem of the town incorporates the arms of Edward the Confessor, those of Leofric, and of the See of Exeter.

Holiday travel started to resume after world hostilities ended in 1945, with massive growth in holiday trade during the 1950s. This generated huge business for the newly formed British Railways and remained through the early 1960s. By the 1970s, the town and surrounding area was starting major change; the annual UK holiday was becoming a thing of the past, with low-cost, easily-accessible air travel tempting the previous UK holidaymaker to seek pastures new. Hotels started to close and be demolished, to be replaced by retirement and second home accommodation, to such an extent that today Dawlish has just one hotel of merit!

The guesthouse market was also adversely affected by the changing holiday patterns, with properties sold off for cheap one-room letting, while others were demolished and rebuilt as high-price nursing homes. The vast majority of remaining holiday accommodation in the area now concentrates on huge camp sites offering a range of packages from self-catering holidays to sites to pitch your own caravan or tent. It is said that the camp sites in and around Dawlish, Dawlish Warren, Starcross and Teignmouth offer a staggering 20,000 beds.

In Dawlish a number of pubs now offer bed and breakfast accommodation while a number of private houses have been turned into holiday lets.

The changing scene of Dawlish has done little for the shops and traders. Like many smaller towns Dawlish now has a wide selection of charity shops with few sole traders remaining. Today, for anything but the basic needs, residents have to travel to larger cities and towns such as Exeter or Newton Abbot to obtain their shopping, much as it was five generations ago! ■

Below: Storming out of Kennaway Tunnel and starting to skirt Marine Parade towards Dawlish station, 'Hall' 4-6-0 No. 6964 Lotherton Hall *leads the 10.06 Summer Saturday Teignmouth to Bradford service on 4 June 1949. The cliff face of Lea Mount is now largely overgrown, a more modern concrete footbridge crosses the railway and many of the buildings have been rendered rather than have exposed brickwork. New fencing now exists on both sides and all but one of the sea wall seats have been removed in the name of safety.* **E. D. Bruton**

Dawlish Seafront and Tunnels

Above: *An amazing image of Dawlish from the Lea Mount footbridge looking towards the station in around 1921, shows a GWR ex-ROD 2-8-0 No. 3004 heading west with a freight duty. This view can easily be repeated today with just a few changes on the left side to buildings along Marine Parade.* **F. H. Stingemore /Rail Archive Stephenson**

Below: *For many years when the two routes to Plymouth were open, one Southern service each day operated by way of the Great Western route west of Exeter, giving the sight of Bulleid Pacific locos on the sea wall. Dated 1949, this image records 'West Country' No. 34001 Exeter departing from Dawlish with a Plymouth-bound express.* **John Bamsey**

Above: *An illustration that we can date to between June and November 1902, as this was the only time GWR prototype two-cylinder 4-6-0 No. 100 carried the name* Dean. *Passing adjacent to the then brand new King's Walk and running on the single line section, No. 100 departs from Dawlish with what is considered to be the daily 06.15 Bristol Temple Meads to Newton Abbot mail train. Just note how many seats are provided along the King's Walk - 12 compared to today's one.* **CJM-C**

Below: *Crossing the Colonnade Viaduct and passing Jubilee Gardens on the approach to Dawlish station, maroon 'Western' No. D1009* Western Invader *heads a train towards Exeter on 23 July 1969. This is another view which has not changed a great deal over the years. The brook, fountain, and gardens are much the same today, except we now have a wishing well on the right bank of the water.* **Bernard Mills**

Above: *Emerging from Kennaway Tunnel and running parallel with Marine Parade, three-car Class 150/9 set No. 150925 slows for its Dawlish stop on 6 April 2015 forming the 11.15 Paignton to Exmouth service. The three-car set, usually deployed in the Bristol area, was being used from Exeter depot over the Easter holiday period to cope with extra traffic levels.* **CJM**

Below: *The railway along the sea wall is signalled for bi-directional operation over the 'up' line between Dawlish Warren and Teignmouth. Normal signalling applies for trains to be crossed over at Dawlish Warren to operate wrong line, allowing some interesting pictures of two westbound trains running side by side if a photographer is lucky. On 27 November 2011, the FGW Class 142 farewell tour was booked to run wrong line between Dawlish Warren and Teignmouth and is seen heading towards Kennaway Tunnel, formed of sets Nos. 142001, 142063 and 142068 en route to Heathfield via Newton Abbot.* **CJM**

Above: *Running between King's Walk on one side and Marine Parade on the other, this classic view of Dawlish sea front was taken on 1 May 1969 from high above the railway on Lea Mount. The westbound train is powered by Class 42 'Warship' No. D820 Grenville. If this and more recent images, such as the one reproduced bottom right of the Marine Parade area, are compared a number of changes have taken place to the buildings. A new block of flats, Burns Court, has been erected where the garage block is shown on the far left, the covered-in roof garden of the original Gentleman's Club has now been opened out as part of Oceans guest house, and the majority of houses have lost their gardens in favour of off-road parking.* **Bernard Mills**

Left: *Several years ago the classic ornate wrought iron fencing which once protected the railway from Marine Parade was replaced by steel fencing, with a low wall built at the base of the fence. With the old GW fencing in situ, 'Western' Class 52 No. D1061 Western Envoy heads towards Dawlish station with train 1A65, the 15.55 Paignton to Paddington, on 9 June 1973.* **Bernard Mills**

Above: *Although not originally a Western Region locomotive, the Class 50s will always be remembered for their work along the scenic South Devon coast line, attracting hundreds of enthusiasts to the area. On 3 July 1982, the pioneer of the fleet No. 50050 (D400) pulls out of Dawlish with the 11.25 Paddington to Plymouth service, formed of Mk2 stock.* **CJM**

Below: *Although the Exeter to Newton Abbot line is out on an extremity of the main line railway system, it does see a large variety of different train types, loco classes and unusual trains; very few weeks pass without something interesting happening. For the summer of 2010 the sea wall route had added interest, when First Great Western hired in a loco and stock formation to cover the 08.00 Cardiff to Paignton and 12.48 return due to a shortage of DMU stock. The train was operated by 'top and tail' Class 67s with four Mk2 coaches coupled between. Led by EWS Management-liveried Class 67 No. 67029 and with No. 67022 on the rear, the 08.00 from Cardiff pulls away from its Dawlish stop on 3 May 2010.* **CJM**

Above: *One of the more picturesque parts of Dawlish seafront is around Boat Cove, at the foot of Lea Mount, where still today local fisherman land their catch. The area around this small harbour offers some excellent viewpoints of the railway, allowing photographers to get a wide picture from the sea side of the line. Two of First Great Western's picture-branded power cars, No. 43163 advertising Plymouth and 43146 supporting Building a Greater West branding, head west on 8 April 2015 with the 09.06 Paddington to Plymouth service.* **CJM**

Below: *The UK's only Turkish-built locomotive, Class 70 No. 70801, emerges from Kennaway Tunnel on 1 April 2014 with a ballast train from Teignmouth which had been involved in final repairs of the sea wall and the Teignmouth land slip before the route reopened to passenger services on 4 April. This was one of the first trains to traverse the 'up' line following the sea wall collapse in February 2014. A number of the US-built Class 70s, which were not delivered when the sea wall collapsed, were commissioned and used to power repair trains before it re-opened.* **CJM**

Above: *In 2009-2011 Freightliner Heavy Haul operated a number of sand trains from Burngullow to London terminals, the sand being a bi-product from the china clay industry and loaded into box wagons in sidings at the east end of the ECC sidings at Burngullow. Due to the weight of the loaded train, even with one of the high-output Class 66/6s the train had to operate over the Devon banks in two sections. With the full load of empties on 6 April 2010, Class 66/6 No. 66624 heads towards Kennaway Tunnel with additional train 6Z16, the 11.21 Crawley to Hackney Yard (Newton Abbot) empty box wagons bound for Burngullow.* **CJM**

Right: *In the days when 'Warship' Class 42 or 43 locos operated the cross-country services, Class 42 No. D808 Centaur pulls out of Kennaway Tunnel on 23 July 1969 with the 12.45 Penzance to Liverpool Lime Street service. The scenic walkway on and above Lea Mount can be seen behind.* **Bernard Mills**

Top: *The annual Dawlish Air Show brings around 100,000 people to the small seaside town. Extra trains are usually run, and for the 2014 event on 23 August, FGW deployed recently named power car No. 43155* Red Arrows *on the west end of one of two extra shuttle trains. The train departs from Dawlish as the 16.16 Exeter to Newton Abbot.* **CJM**

Above: *The Air Show on 20 August 2009 saw FGW provide a loco-hauled extra train, using two Class 67s and four Mk2s. The train is seen approaching Dawlish formed of No. 67005 with No. 67025 on the rear as the 12.15 Newton Abbot to Exeter.* **CJM**

Left: *A special fly-over by the RAF Red Arrows at Dawlish on 22 August 2014.* **CJM**

Below: *Class 180 No. 180106 was provided for the Air Show day shuttle service on 17 August 2006. The set departs Dawlish as the 11.28 Newton Abbot to Exeter.* **CJM**

Above: *For the Dawlish Air Show, every inch of space from Dawlish Warren to the hills west of Dawlish is crammed with people. This was the view from the top of Langstone Rock for the 2014 event on 23 August, and shows FGW Plymouth-liveried advertising power car No. 43163 leading the 10.00 Penzance to Paddington.* **Antony Christie**

Below: *Little space appears to be left on the main beach at Dawlish on 14 August 2003 as people get ready for the Air Show. In the days before the railway supported the event and operated extra trains, two-car Wessex Trains Class 150/2 No. 150261 departs from its Dawlish call forming the 13.54 Exmouth to Paignton service. It is a major logistical nightmare to try and shift the number of people visiting Dawlish on Air Show day; these days a queuing system operates at the station for late afternoon departing trains.* **CJM**

Above: *One of the more spectacular views of Lyme Bay including Dawlish right round to Langstone Rock is from the fields to the west of the town overlooking Clerks Tunnel and Horse Cove. Until recently the coastal footpath, crossing fields from Old Teignmouth Road heading west, went close to the fence and photographers could obtain stunning views of trains emerging from the tunnel. However, under Health & Safety regulations a tall steel fence has now been erected all but stopping this view of the countryside. On 20 May 2006, former Central Trains Class 158 No. 158793 is seen between Clerks and Parsons Tunnels, forming the 12.54 Exmouth to Paignton service.* **CJM**

Below: *From the start of privatisation until the December 2009 timetable change, South West Trains operated a skeleton through service to Paignton, Plymouth and on Sundays to Penzance. These were formed of Class 159 stock, but following the need to operate extra SWT services on their core route, the through trains to the west beyond Exeter ceased. On 17 June 2006, Class 159/0 No. 159006 emerges from Clerks Tunnel and passes Horse Cove with the 09.57 Brighton to Paignton via Salisbury and Exeter service.* **CJM**

Above: *With a low tide exposing the rocks, a red and silver liveried Virgin Trains 'Voyager' passes Horse Cove, providing a scene which cannot be repeated. Although many do not like the travelling experience of the Bombardier-built 'Voyager' sets, they were colourful and made an interesting subject to photograph. On 18 April 2007, set No. 220012* Lanarkshire Voyager *forms the 08.24 Newcastle to Paignton service.* **CJM**

Below: *In the days of loco-hauled summer Saturday trains, Horse Cove was an excellent and popular location to sit and wait for the action. On 5 August 1989 Class 31s Nos. 31425 and 31314 power the 09.33 Stockport to Paignton out of Clerks Tunnel.* **CJM**

Dawlish Fights the Elements

Above: *It is nothing new to experience inclement weather along the South Devon coast, especially in the Dawlish and Teignmouth area. Going back in history many reports have been made of line blockages, closure and wash-outs, some more serious than others. The 'down' platform at Dawlish station has had to be repaired numerous times and will likely have to be in the future. The route between Dawlish Warren and Teignmouth is signalled for bi-directional running over the 'up' line, allowing trains to work on the landward track in both directions during rough seas. This view shows the storm force seas on the morning of 23 January 2007 when single-line working was in operation. EWS Class 66 No. 66061 heads west with the overnight Irvine to Burngullow empty china clay train.* **CJM**

Filmstrip Right: *Storms at Dawlish between 2000 and 2014. All:* **CJM**

Left: *The results on the 'down' platform of a storm on 11 February 1974, where the sea ripped up the platform decking and destroyed the wood back fence. With the open sea wall and walkway below, there was, and still is, little to protect the 'down' platform.* **John A. M. Vaughan**

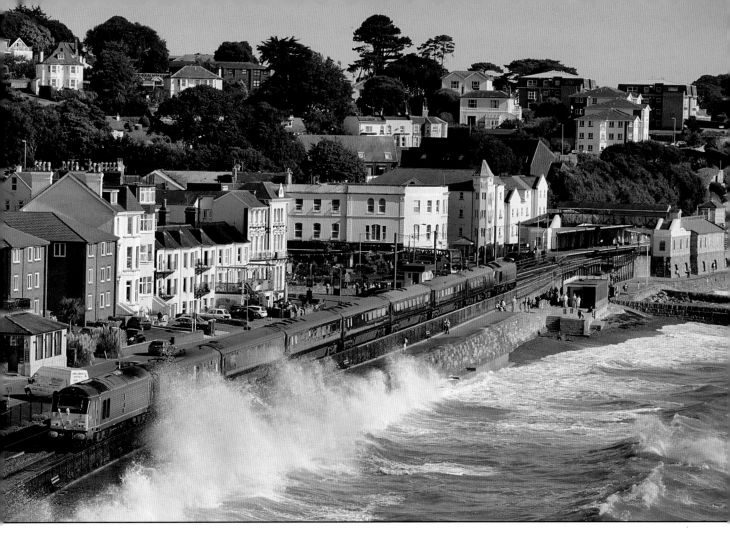

Above: *The rough sea is not fussy about what train it douses in water! On 11 September 2009 the full Royal Train heads west along the sea wall 'topped and tailed' by Class 67s Nos. 67006 and 67005 forming the 10.05 Exeter to Hackney Yard empty stock move.* **CJM**

Right: *Looking west from Dawlish station on 13 November 2014, a westbound CrossCountry HST battles towards Kennaway Tunnel with waves breaking over the train and landing in Marine Parade. In the foreground the track is covered by froth, stirred up where the rough sea meets the outlet of the Dawlish Water.* **Simon Thurgood**

Right Bottom: *With a huge amount of sea water rolling off the track and draining off King's Walk, two-car Class 150/2 No. 150253 makes slow progress away from Dawlish on 21 September 2006 with the 17.54 Exmouth-Paignton.* **CJM**

Below: *After the February 1974 storm, very little was left of the wooden section of the down platform at Dawlish, as seen from a passing train. It is surprising that the line was still open.* **John A. M. Vaughan**

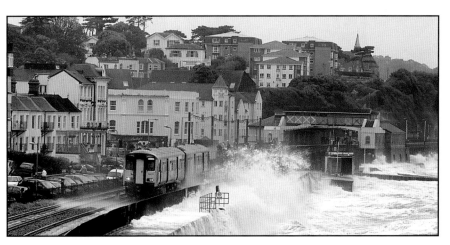

Teignmouth Sea Wall

Above: *The view looking towards Teignmouth from Sprey point, mid-way along the Teignmouth Sea Wall, is a charming view with the parish church of St Michaels in the background. On 18 March 2015, 'Super Voyager' No. 221124 heads away from Teignmouth with train 1S43, the 06.28 Penzance to Glasgow Central.* **CJM**

Left: *On 22 June 1974, in the days when four-character headcodes were still in use and Teignmouth mechanical signal box was still open, 'Peak' No. 45115 heads west towards Teignmouth station with the 08.08 Wolverhampton to Penzance service.* **CJM**

Below: *An original Great Western Railway wooden milepost 208, mounted on a rail post on the sea wall at Teignmouth.* **CJM**

Above: *The most iconic photographic location along the Teignmouth Sea Wall section is Skew Bridge, where Eastcliffe Walk passes over the railway, at the Exeter end of Teignmouth station, and where the railway turns to follow the coastline through to Dawlish Warren. Advertising FGW power car No. 43146 emerges from under the bridge on 18 March 2015 leading the 07.41 Penzance to Paddington.* **CJM**

Below: *The Skew Bridge image has hardly changed over the years, apart from the lack of semaphore signalling today, more vegetation and wooden protection boards on the cliff side to protect the line from rock falls. On 2 July 1959, 'Warship' No. D805* Benbow *leads the 07.15 Plymouth to Paddington.* **R. Dobson**

Above: *On 4 March 1952, gas-turbine loco No. 18100 heads towards Parsons Tunnel on the Teignmouth Sea Wall section with a returning test run from Swindon to Plymouth. The walker on the sea wall looks on with amazement at this non-steam-powered train traverses the line.* **CJM-C**

Left Top: *Ministry of Supply 2-8-0 No. 77388 runs along the Teignmouth Sea Wall towards Parsons Tunnel on 2 June 1949 with a potato train from Bodmin to London.* **E. D. Bruton**

Left Bottom: *With the Coach House off Holcombe Drive dominating the horizon above Parsons Tunnel, Class 50 No. 50020* Revenge *trundles west towards Sprey Point on 30 September 1980 with a short unfitted freight.* **CJM**

Below: *Although the sea wall route was not in the Network SouthEast area, trains in the red, white and blue livery were frequently seen in the area, being based at Laira depot and working through services. On 15 July 1989, Class 50 No. 50017* Royal Oak *approaches Parsons Tunnel with a full NSE-liveried train forming the 09.33 Plymouth to Brighton service.* **Bernard Mills**

Left: *The storms, huge waves and rain, which caused havoc at Dawlish in February 2014, also caused considerable damage to the cliff between Parsons Tunnel and Sprey Point, Teignmouth, as well as massive structural damage to the walkway, slipways and sea wall. These were largely repaired concurrent with the two-month line closure, but the stablisation of the embankment is an ongoing issue. In the area of the greatest problem, movement sensors have been installed to give warning of movement before damage can occur. The embankment is shown in the main picture and one of the solar-powered sensors in the inset image. Both:* **CJM**

Below: *Major damage was caused to the low wall separating the rail line from the walkway, with much of it washed away. A new concrete wall with stone-style facing has now been built which should weather to a more mellow colour as time progresses. This is a section close to the Dawlish end of Sprey point.* **CJM**

Above Left: *One of the new single display light emitting diode (LED) signals installed on the sea wall, with one 'light' able to show the different required aspects.* **CJM**

Left: *When the cliff face collapsed in February 2014, huge amounts of water was sprayed on and injected into the face to induce a rock/mud fall to quicken up the process of clearing away the problem. Once stablised, netting was fitted to the cliff face and a protection barrier built, fitted with movement sensors to give warning of problems which could affect safe train operation. On 18 March 2015, Class 143s Nos. 143620 and 143621 pass the eroded cliff forming train 2F17, the 09.13 Paignton to Exmouth.* **CJM**

Britain's Scenic Railways Dawlish - The Railway from Exeter to Newton Abbot

Above: *The present brick portal at the west end of the 512 yard (468m) Parsons Tunnel was built with the doubling of the track in 1905, and is said to be the best looking of the 10 tunnel portals between Dawlish and Teignmouth. On 26 June 1977, then un-named Class 50 No. 50015 storms out the portal with the 07.30 Paddington to Penzance.* **CJM**

Below: *Making a colourful sight pulling away from Parsons Tunnel, South West Trains Class 159s Nos. 159015 and 159002 form the 08.35 Waterloo to Paignton via Exeter St Davids service on 6 April 2002. Steps at the end of the public walkway here lead to a path under the railway and Smugglers Lane leading to the main Teignmouth-Dawlish Road.* **CJM**

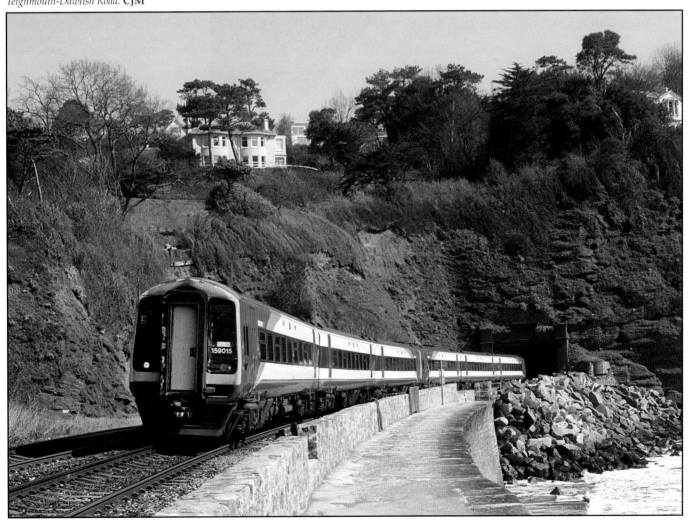

Teignmouth Station and Docks

Above: *The present station at Teignmouth was built in 1895 to replace a South Devon structure dating from 1846. The 1895 structure was much like other GWR resort stations at Weston-super-Mare and Torquay. The main station buildings are on the 'down' westbound platform, linked to the 'up' platform by a footbridge. Until June 1965 a goods yard existed on the 'up' side behind the station buildings, and this continued to handle coal until December 1967 when it closed. The site is now industrial units. Today the station is served by First Great Western Exmouth to Paignton line services with a handful of main-line FGW and CrossCountry trains. This is the view of the outside of the main station building looking from the west, showing the spring 2015 condition.* **CJM**

Left Middle & Left Below: *Views of the 'up' platform and buildings from the westbound platform; the middle view is looking east and shows the rather decrepit footbridge, while the lower view is looking west.* **CJM**

Above: *Teignmouth station in its heyday. On Saturday 11 June 1949, the 'up' Saturdays only 08.35 Falmouth to Paddington express, which the timetable shows ran non-stop from Plymouth to Paddington, storms through Teignmouth under clear signals powered by 'Castle' No. 4081* Warwick Castle. *The first coach behind the locomotive is a Great Western 'toplight'.* **E. D. Bruton**

Right: *With Teignmouth being a slightly larger town than Dawlish in terms of permanent residence, 20,000 compared to 16,000 for Dawlish, the annual passenger return reflects this increase. In common with the route the passenger figures have doubled in the period 2002-2003 to 2012-2013. This is likely to reflect local travel rather than holiday and seasonal use, with few hotels in Teignmouth and the majority of holidaymakers now opting for road transport. The sea wall collapse glitch can be seen in the 2013-2014 figures.*

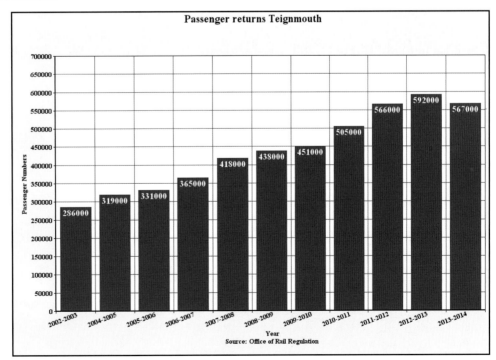

Passenger returns Teignmouth

Year	Passenger Numbers
2002-2003	286000
2004-2005	319000
2005-2006	331000
2006-2007	365000
2007-2008	418000
2008-2009	438000
2009-2010	451000
2010-2011	505000
2011-2012	566000
2012-2013	592000
2013-2014	567000

Source: Office of Rail Regulation

Britain's Scenic Railways Dawlish - The Railway from Exeter to Newton Abbot

With Our Lady and St Patrick's Roman Catholic Church towering above the cutting to the east of Teignmouth station, First Great Western 'bubble' Class 153 No. 153377 departs from the station on 18 March 2015 forming the 10.33 Paignton to Exeter St Davids. Great Western Railway have said that following introduction of electric trains in the London area in 2017-19, and a 'shuffle' of rolling stock, the Class 143s and 153s from the Exeter division will be withdrawn, replaced by further Class 150 and 158 stock. **CJM**

Viewed looking east from the top of Skew Bridge, the Teignmouth Sea Wall is seen leading around the tight curve towards Sprey Point and Parsons Tunnel. The land directly ahead is the Parson and Clerk rock, with the residential housing to the left being part of the village of Holcombe. The train is a Westbury to Moorswater cement service, powered by Class 66/6 No. 66613 on 27 March 2012. **CJM**

Along the banks of the River Teign

Above: *After departing from Teignmouth, the railway starts to skirt the River Teign for its run to Newton Abbot. After passing Teignmouth Docks and passing below Shaldon Bridge, it progresses past the village of Bishopsteignton. On 25 July 1935, prototype streamlined Great Western 'King' No. 6014* King Henry VII *is seen between Bishopsteignton and Teignmouth with a Newquay to Paddington express.* **CJM-C**

Below: *A good photographic viewpoint for both 'up' and 'down' trains is Shaldon Bridge, the main road linking Teignmouth with Shaldon and Ringmoor. Today, a shallow fence impedes some of the view, but it is still popular with photographers. With the Port of Teignmouth in the background, 'Peak' Class 45 No. 45026 approaches Shaldon Bridge on 2 August 1979, powering train 6V33, the 04.24 Stoke-on-Trent to St Blazey.* **Bernard Mills**

Above: *The view looking west from Shaldon Bridge sees trains curving around from the Teignmouth boat yard; again in recent years a safety fence has been erected, but this does not interfere with a picture of an 'up' train. On 20 May 2006, EWS Class 66/0 No. 66077* Benjamin Gimbert GC *approaches Shaldon Bridge with the 11.05 Plymouth to Taunton VSOE lunch special, part of an annual visit the Orient Express train makes to Devon and Cornwall.* **CJM**

Below: *The Swindon-built cross-country DMU stock did operate frequently in the west in later years, when classified under BR TOPS as Class 120. However, in this view recorded on 3 May 1959, two three-car sets approach Shaldon Bridge forming an excursion train bound for Torquay and Paignton.* **David Sellman**

This superb panoramic vista looking over west Teignmouth from high above Shaldon, shows the area west of Shaldon Bridge towards the boat yard and the Broadmeadow Industrial area. The train is rather unusual, as it consists of a pair of FGW power cars, Nos. 43030 and 43094, hauling failed Direct Rail Services Class 57 No. 57310 Pride of Cumbria, the First Great Western 'Night Riviera' sleeper and seating stock, plus FGW Class 57/6 No. 57602 Restormel Castle dead on the rear. This most unusual formation operated following the failure of the previous night's 'up' sleeper train, followed by the failure of the assisting loco.
Nathan Williamson

Britain's Scenic Railways Dawlish - The Railway from Exeter to Newton Abbot

Above: *Passing the Hackney, Newton Abbot, home signal in February 1968, a Rail Blue-liveried Birmingham RC&W Class 118 three-car set heads towards Newton Abbot with a stopping service from Exeter. The buildings in the background are the village of Bishopsteignton.* **Bernard Mills**

Left Top: *With the village of Bishopsteignton in the background, this is the view looking west from a small footbridge crossing the line near the village allowing access to the banks of the River Teign, and providing access to a couple of riverside houses. On 7 July 1984, Class 47/3 No. 47311 passes, powering the 10.20 Paignton to Glasgow service.* **CJM**

Left Below: *Preserved steam locos No. 4965 Rood Ashton Hall and No. 5043 Earl of Mount Edgcumbe pass Wear Farm alongside the River Teign on 15 May 2010 forming the 07.01 Birmingham Snow Hill to Plymouth 'The Cornishman' charter.* **Antony Christie**

Right Middle: *A train which ran from the steam era to 2013 was the depot fuel service from Fawley to Plymouth. On 17 April 2007 the train approaches Newton Abbot at Hackney Marsh powered by EWS Class 66/0 No. 66242. This loco is now one of the batch operating in France.* **Antony Christie**

Right Bottom: *Hackney Yard is located just at the Exeter end of Newton Abbot station, opposite Newton Abbot race course. It was once a busy freight and ballast facility, but in recent years has seen a reduced workload. For several years it was a staging point for Freightliner cement traffic to Cornwall and recently has been a rail reclamation facility. On 12 April 2005, Freightliner No. 66614 is seen in the yard with a cement train bound for Moorswater.* **CJM**

Newton Abbot to Aller Junction

Above: *Today, Newton Abbot station is but a shadow of the past; all that remains are three through platform lines, plus the old Moretonhampstead bay, sometimes used for stabling a locomotive. In the days when the thriving market town's station was more busy, Class 52 'Western' No. D1064* Western Regent *awaits the signal in the 'up' main platform on 20 April 1974 with an afternoon Penzance to Paddington express. On the right a Class 120 Swindon cross-country DMU awaits its next duty.* **Bernard Mills**

Below: *A wonderful period image of Newton Abbot. Newton Abbot power station can be seen behind the train, a mass of semaphore signals exist, and a covered-in Motorail van from the Eastern Region can be seen poking out in front of the 'Warship'. Recorded on 1 December 1970, Class 43 'Warship' No. D843* Sharpshooter *pilots Class 47 No. 1553 with the northbound 'Devonian' from Paignton to Bradford.* **Bernard Mills**

Newton Abbot

Right Top: *Newton Abbot station, located at the end of Queen Street about a quarter of a mile from the town centre, is a stunning building. It was constructed in 1927 as a replacement for a previous structure slightly to the east. The building housed a booking and information office and all station facilities with sizable office accommodation on the two upper floors. The ground floor of the building is still used today as the booking and information office. In more recent years the building has been named 'South Devon House'. The building was heavily refurbished in 2014. This image was taken in 2015.* **CJM**

Right Middle: *In its heyday, Newton Abbot station had non-platform through lines, on which freight traffic and non-stop passenger services would pass. On 5 August 1971, 'Warship' No. D831 Monarch passes Newton Abbot on the 'up' through line with freight 7B81 from Tavistock Junction to Exeter Riverside.* **David Wharton**

Right Bottom: *In 2015 Newton Abbot saw around 1.2million passenger returns, increasing from under 640,000 11 years earlier. This is a significant increase in rail journeys and reflects the general trend for the South West's rail economy. Newton Abbot has for many years been a main passenger point for those from the Dartmoor area who use the station as a hub, rather than the longer drive to Exeter. However, today Totnes, with its good rail service, has taken some of the Newton customer base. In common with all other stations in the area the slight downturn in customers in 2013-14 was due to the sea wall problems, and is expected to recover to previous growth levels in the 2014-15 year.*

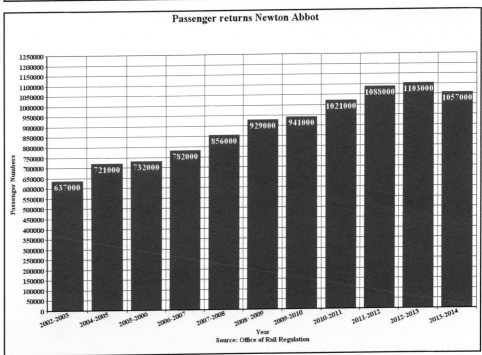

Passenger returns Newton Abbot

Year	Passenger Numbers
2002-2003	637000
2004-2005	721000
2005-2006	732000
2006-2007	782000
2007-2008	856000
2008-2009	929000
2009-2010	941000
2010-2011	1021000
2011-2012	1088000
2012-2013	1103000
2013-2014	1057000

Source: Office of Rail Regulation

Left Top: *Newton Abbot platforms. Platform No. 3, nearest the main entrance, is accessed on the level from the booking hall, while platforms 2 and 3 have to be accessed by a footbridge or lift. All three lines through Newton Abbot are bi-directional and controlled by Exeter Panel Signal Box. Usually 'up' trains use platform 3, 'down' trains use platform 2 and Paignton branch trains use platform 3. This view is looking west from platform 2 towards platform 3.* **CJM**

Left Middle: *Newton Abbot East Signal Box was located at the Exeter end of the station, between the main and Moretonhampstead (Heathfield) lines. The box was opened on 25 April 1926 and had a staggering 206 levers. Over the years the box, and the number of operational levers were rationalised. It was closed on 4 May 1987 under the West of England resignalling project. This view shows the box in July 1956.* **CJM-C**

Below: *Adjacent to Newton Abbot station was Newton Abbot motive power depot and workshops. They both operated through the steam era and continued to maintain diesel-hydraulic traction after the Western Region modernisation. The workshops were a key player in 'Warship', 'Western' and D63xx loco maintenance. In this view inside the work section of the facility a 'Warship' loco receives attention.* **CJM-C**

Right: *With Newton Abbot West Signal Box behind the first coach, 'Western' Class 52 No. D1032* Western Marksman *pulls into Newton Abbot on 6 August 1971 with the 16.30 Plymouth to Paddington service. The track in the foreground was the 'up' through line used by fast passenger and through freight services.*
John Cooper-Smith

Below: *In 2013-15 the reliability of the First Great Western Class 57/6 locos was poor, with Direct Rail Services supplying a hired-in Class 57/3 on most days to cover the shortage. In 2014, after the Network Rail-owned Class 57s had been transferred to DRS, some still painted in Network Rail yellow operated the FGW sleeper services, making an interesting photographic opportunity. On 14 August 2014, the westbound Paddington to Penzance 'Night Riviera' service is seen awaiting the signal from Newton Abbot powered by NR-liveried No. 57305.* **Antony Christie**

To the west of Newton Abbot is Aller, where once a junction, now a divergence, of the Plymouth and Paignton lines is located. Recently, the entire area between Newton Abbot and beyond Aller has been ripped apart by road construction, changing the face of the railway for ever. Passing under the now demolished farm bridge at Aller, Class 37/4 No. 37412 takes the Plymouth line on 9 June 1989 with a Heathfield to St Blazey clay working formed of just three wagons. **CJM**

Left: *The farm bridge, illustrated in the above picture, was a traditional location for railway photographs through the ages, until it was demolished in 2014 to make way for road construction. From the bridge looking east on 4 July 2005, FGW green-liveried Class 57 No. 57605* Totnes Castle *hauls power cars Nos. 43124 and 43189 plus a TGS coach as the 13.45 Bristol St Philips Marsh to Laira stock move.* **Antony Christie**

Below: *During the first period of Class 142 'Skipper' operations in the West Country in the mid-1980s, set No. 142026 departs from Newton Abbot and crosses to the 'down' Paignton line with the 10.20 Exeter St Davids to Paignton on 20 April 1987. During the West of England resignalling work in the Newton Abbot area, which was taking place at the time this picture was recorded, the layout was totally changed west of Newton Abbot with the two routes to Paignton and Plymouth running side by side.* **CJM**

Above: *Passing under the farm bridge at Aller, on what was then the 'down Plymouth' on 13 August 1955, a westbound freight applies power for the start of the arduous climb towards Dainton, headed by Newton Abbot-based 2-6-2T No. 5113 and 'Hall' 4-6-0 No. 7901* Dodington Hall. *The tank loco was withdrawn just two months later.* **T. E. Williams**

Below: *The site once occupied by Aller Junction signal box is now just a parking space for rail maintenance vehicles, and the physical junction of the lines has been moved back to Newton Abbot West, with Aller just being the diverging point of the tracks. Running along the 'up Paignton' on 11 May 1989, which until 1986 was the 'down Plymouth', Laira-allocated Class 108 set No. 955 (51933 and 52054) forms a Paignton to Exeter St Davids stopping service.* **CJM**

Britain's Scenic Railways Dawlish - The Railway from Exeter to Newton Abbot

Left: *What is now referred to as the Heathfield branch is the truncated stump of the original Newton Abbot to Moretonhampstead branch, which closed to passenger traffic in February 1959, and to freight services in April 1964. A few specials did operate after that date, the last being to Bovey Tracey in July 1970. The line was then truncated to Heathfield which continued to handle freight, china clay and oil until 2009 when the line was mothballed. It re-opened at the end of 2011 to handle Kronospan log traffic, which ceased to operate from a loading pad at Teigngrace in spring 2015. On 12 October 1980, Class 118 sets Nos. P470 and P480 stand at Heathfield with the RPPR 'The Mayflower' tour from London to Devon and Cornish branch lines. The train was formed of a loco and Mk1 stock between London and Newton Abbot and return, from where the Class 118s took over.* **CJM**

Above & Left: *As an introductory event to the 1997 celebrations for the 150th anniversary of railways arriving in Newton Abbot, three return trips over the Heathfield branch were organised for 31 December 1996, when EWS Class 37s Nos. 37416 and 37668 'topped and tailed' four coaches. The trains, which operated from the main station at Newton Abbot to the remaining platform at Heathfield, were well loaded, even though it was New Year's Eve. In the above view, catching the low winter sun, EWS-liveried No. 37668 passes Jetty Marsh, where once the sidings into the ball clay works diverged. On the left, the train is seen in the platform at Heathfield. The track continues on towards Moretonhampstead for only a short distance and once served the now long-closed Heltor Ltd oil terminal.* Both: **CJM**

Above: *In the days when a 'down' goods loop still existed on the Plymouth line west of Aller, Class 50 No. 50015* Valiant *powers west with the 15.30 Paddington to Penzance on 23 June 1978.* **CJM**

Right: *In the period when Virgin Trains CrossCountry were operating Class 47-powered Mk2 sets on some services, No. 47805* Pride of Toton *approaches Aller Junction from Dainton incline with the 08.46 Penzance to Manchester on 28 May 2002.* **CJM**

Below: *Taken from Langford Bridge looking east on 24 July 2012, EWS No. 66005 heads the weekly Fawley to Tavistock Junction fuel service.* **Antony Christie**

Teigngrace-Chirk log traffic

Above: *In December 2011 it was announced that the line between Newton Abbot East and Heathfield would be re-opened to facilitate the transport of timber from Teigngrace crossing to the Kronospan wood processing plant in Chirk, North Wales. The timber, in log form, was being supplied by the UK's largest forest harvesting and marketing company, Euroforest, and would be shipped by Colas Rail Freight. Soon after, a timber road-rail transfer site was opened at Teigngrace, adjacent to the level crossing at Exeter Road, allowing logs to be loaded onto the freight trains. As Teigngrace did not have a siding, the trains had to operate via a run-round at Heathfield and then collect their load on the return up the branch to Newton Abbot. Loading of the logs was carried out by road vehicles. The operation commenced on 5 December 2011 and continued infrequently until 2 April 2015 when the loading operation was transferred to Exeter Riverside. In this view, Colas Class 66 No. 66847 passes Rockstone Bridge, Dawlish, on 5 December 2011 with the first westbound empty log train, running as the 09.05 Gloucester New Yard to Teigngrace.* **CJM**

Left Middle: *After a period of using Class 66s on the duty, Class 56s took over in 2012. On 19 September 2012, No. 56094 is seen between Heathfield and Teigngrace with the empty log train.* **Antony Christie**

Left Below: *The loading of the log wagons was a complex affair, with the train having to be loaded in two sections. To do this, the empty train was split in two on the approach to the crossing and the front half drawn forward for loading; when complete the two portions were reattached and the rear section drawn into the loading area. No. 56094 is seen at Teigngrace on 27 September 2012.* **Antony Christie**

Above: *Colas Rail freight was frequently unable to resource the Teigngrace log train and operate it when required by the customer, which was often due to failures of the Class 56s rostered for the duty. On occasions this resulted in the train being double-headed, much to the delight of photographers. On 11 March 2015, Colas Class 56s Nos. 56078 and 56105 head towards Dawlish station with train 6M51, the 08.56 Teigngrace to Chirk, running several hours late.* **CJM**

Below: *By April 2015 it was agreed that loading of the train would transfer to the much easier road-rail transfer site at Exeter Riverside Yard, with the final loaded train operating out of Teigngrace on 2 April. This train is seen pulling out of Kennaway Tunnel powered by Colas Class 70 No. 70804 operating as the 08.56 Teigngrace to Chirk running 99 minutes late. After transfer to Exeter, this train was operated by Colas Rail Freight Class 60 locomotives.* **CJM**

Steam Charter Services

Above: *For well over 30 years the railway route west from Exeter has been on the steam charter circuit, with frequent steam charters operating at weekends, and in more recent years on some weekdays. The main west destinations for steam-powered trains are Paignton/Kingswear, Plymouth and Par, where locos can be turned with relative ease. On 26 June 2010 Steam Dreams operated their 'Cornish Riviera' charter which started from Paddington powered by King No. 6024* King Edward I *as far as Taunton, from where it was piloted to Exeter by 'Western' No. D1015* Western Champion. *Forward from Exeter to Par the train was double-headed by No. 6024* King Edward I *and No. 5029* Nunney Castle *which are seen approaching Kennaway Tunnel from the roof of a property in Marine Parade, Dawlish.* **CJM**

Left: *For a few years in the late 1990s 'The Dawlish Donkey' steam service was operated by Past Time Rail, with three return trips for several days in the summer between Exeter and Newton Abbot; powered by Great Western 1400 class 0-4-2T No. 1450. As no turning facility was available at Newton Abbot, the train operated in an easterly direction 'bunker first'. Formed of four carriages, it is seen rounding the curve onto the sea wall at Langstone Rock, Dawlish Warren, on 13 April 1998 forming the 09.50 Exeter St Davids to Newton Abbot.* **CJM**

Above: *Whenever steam charters operate along the sea wall section, no matter what the weather, huge crowds gather to see and photograph their passing. This is usually a mix of locals and visitors. It is amazing how many rail enthusiasts have moved to Dawlish due to the presence of the railway. A locomotive which always attracts a large following is 'new' steam loco No. 60163* Tornado, *which has traversed the sea wall on many occasions. On 8 August 2009, painted in apple green, No. 60163 heads through Dawlish, passing below the old footbridge, with charter 1Z60, the 06.36 Birmingham New Street to Plymouth, 'The Tamar Tornado', organised by Pathfinder Tours.* **CJM**

Right: *A Southern-Great Western combination operated over the sea wall on 5 September 2014, when Bulleid 'West Country No. 34046* Braunton *piloted GW No. 5029* Nunney Castle *on the 16.45 Exeter St Davids to Penzance Steam Dreams charter 'The Atlantic Coast Express'. The train is seen skirting Marine Parade making the slight turn before entering Kennaway Tunnel.* **CJM**

Dawlish Station Footbridge Renewal

Above: For a long time the deteriorating condition of the footbridge linking the platforms at Dawlish station was causing concern. In 2012 it was replaced by Network Rail over the weekend of 13/14 October, when in conjunction Tony Gee, Civil Engineers and Bam-Nuttall carried out a major engineering operation. The Grade II listed station with its 57ft 6in (17.5m) covered steel footbridge, modernised in 1937, had deteriorated beyond repair. Its replacement was a lightweight structure weighing only 5 tonnes, one third of the original bridge. Designed by Tony Gee and Optima Projects, the new structure used modern advanced materials technology and was the first Fibre Reinforced Polymer (FRP) composite bridge installed at a station. The new structure closely replicated the character of the original bridge. The structure was installed by Bam-Nuttall and fabricated by Pipex Structural Composites. In the weeks leading up to the installation of the new bridge the old one was removed and a temporary entrance built from the sea wall to the down platform. **CJM**

Left: The new pre-formed 'plastic' bridge was delivered to Dawlish station on a King Lifting lorry during the afternoon of 13 October and installed by road crane overnight. **Antony Christie**

Above: *The overnight engineering work at Dawlish station to install the new footbridge was completed at dawn on 14 October 2012 and the station and line returned to the operators, with a normal service running. Although installed, the footbridge was not put into use for several weeks, as it had to be finally adjusted, the steps made to fit, and electrical work completed. One of the first trains to pass below the new bridge was Freightliner Class 66/5 No. 66511 with a loaded Network Rail rail train from Bedwyn to Hackney Yard, Newton Abbot.* **CJM**

Right: *The new bridge deck as opened to the public, using LED downlighting. Sadly this failed and has now been replaced with some very basic plastic cover florescent lights, tied on to the purpose-built lighting assembly with plastic clips.* **CJM**

Below: *To provide walking access to the 'down' westbound platform while the footbridge was closed and removed, a temporary scaffold stair was built at the country end of the platform, with a temporary tarmac surface over the stone walkway provided under the station overhang.* **CJM**

Unusual Trains on the Sea Wall

Above: *The sea wall route always seems to attract a large number of unusual and interesting train movements, and there is hardly a week without some unusual train in the area. Always pleasing to observe and photograph are the Network Rail test trains. On 17 June 2014, an almost 54-year-old Class 31/1 No. 31233 was captured passing adjacent to Marine Parade hauling vehicles Nos. 977986, 977985, 62384 and 9708 as test train 3Q01, the 17.06 Exeter Riverside to Exeter Riverside via Paignton, Goodrington, Heathfield and Barnstaple.* **CJM**

Below: *A frequent visitor to the sea wall is the New Measurement Train (NMT) which usually makes a visit on a Friday morning working a circuit from London Old Oak Common to Plymouth and return, before working back to its main base at Derby. On 20 June 2014, the NMT heads west along the sea wall running as train 1Q18, the 05.17 Old Oak Common to Plymouth via Paddington. The train is 'topped and tailed' by power cars Nos. 43062 and 43014.* **CJM**

Above & Below: *The transfer of empty stock to and from Laira depot, Plymouth, especially HST stock, can cause something of a problem, as the vehicles do not have conventional draw gear and require the use of a barrier or coupling adapter. On 8 July 2010 when GBRf were contracted to transport off-lease buffer cars No. 40736, 40725, 40726, 40744, 40738, 40709 and 40745 from Laira to Eastleigh Works, a special arrangement had to be made, as the two usual barrier vehicles were not available. GBRf used Class 73s Nos. 73206 and 73212 to act as barriers, as these were fitted with buck-eye couplings at one end and could attach to the HST stock. Class 66 No. 66729, hauling the two electro-diesels, arrived at Laira the evening before and formed up the train which departed on the morning on 8 July 2010 formed of Class 66 No. 66729, Class 73 No. 73206, the Mk3 stock and ED No. 73212 on the rear. This most unusual train, forming the 10.00 Laira to Eastleigh Works, is seen from both front and back passing Rockstone Bridge, Dawlish. Both:* **CJM**

Above & Below: *Most years the Royal Train traverses the Exeter to Newton Abbot line at least twice. The train, usually kept at Wolverton Works and used only by the Queen, Prince Philip and Prince of Wales, is often the preferred method of transport to the West Country for early morning visits, with the passengers able to have a good night's rest on board. Normally the train operates from Euston in London and frequently, depending on its final destination, recesses overnight at the bottom end of the Heathfield branch, Newton Abbot, especially if engagements are in Plymouth or further west. After the passengers have been dropped off, the train normally returns empty to Wolverton. On 20 March 2015, when the Queen visited Plymouth to inspect HMS* Ocean, *she travelled west on the Royal Train, which in these images is seen returning empty, as train 1Z40, the 11.07 Plymouth to Wolverton; from the front the train was formed of Class 67 No. 67005* Royal Sovereign, *Royal saloons Nos. 2920, 2915, 2917, 2923, 2904, 2903 and 2921 with Class 67 No. 67026* Diamond Jubilee *coupled on the rear. The train is seen passing Rockstone Bridge. Both:* **CJM**

Britain's Scenic Railways Dawlish - The Railway from Exeter to Newton Abbot

Above & Right: *Most years a couple of MoD high-capacity nuclear flask trains are recorded on the sea wall section, travelling between BNFL Sellafield and the Royal Navy Dockyard at Plymouth, operated by Direct Rail Services. Normally when the flask wagons are loaded, escort coaches accompany the load. On 10 September 2010, DRS Class 37 No. 37059 passes Dawlish Warren with the 04.36 Crewe Coal Yard to Keyham, formed of flask wagons Nos. MODA95770 and MODA95771. Flask wagon MODA95770 is shown right. Both:* **CJM**

Below: *The first time a pair of Class 20s had been used to power the Plymouth flask train was on 1 May 2012, when Nos. 20303 and 20312 powered the 05.10 Crewe to Keyham, formed of flask wagon No. MODA95770, and support coaches Nos. 9428 and 9419. The train is seen passing Dawlish station.* **CJM**

Left Top: *It is not uncommon to see pairs of First Great Western power cars working along the sea wall section, usually operating 'light power' between the main FGW depots at Laira (Plymouth), St Philips Marsh (Bristol), Old Oak Common (London) and Landore (Swansea). However, it is very rare to find single power cars running on their own. On 27 May 2014, Class 43 No. 43003 Isambard Kingdom Brunel pulls away from Kennaway Tunnel running as 0Z74, the 13.28 Laira to St Philips Marsh.* **CJM**

Left Middle: *Modern digital photographic equipment now allows night photography of moving trains by using high recording speed and suitable noise-reduction software. Recorded at 21.20 on 12 January 2014, Aggregate Industries Class 59/0 No. 59005 Kenneth J Painter powers the 18.16 Westbury to Burngullow empty MRL bogie box wagons for loading with sand.* **CJM**

Below: *For several years on Summer Saturdays, one of the Great North Eastern Railway and later National Express East Coast HST sets was hired to CrossCountry to provide extra capacity for West of England holiday traffic. On 8 September 2009, National Express East Coast power cars Nos. 43277 and 43312 with a nine-car trailer set pass Dawlish with the 07.00 Manchester Piccadilly to Newquay.* **CJM**

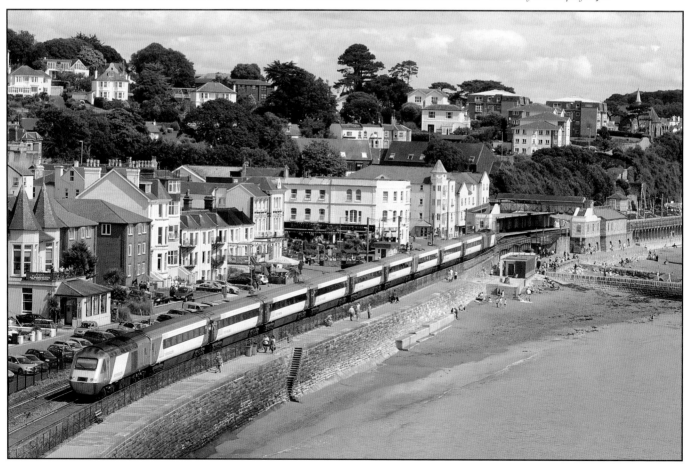

Above: *Each year between October and mid-December, Network Rail operate a number of Rail Head Treatment Trains (RHTTs) which blast water onto the rail head to clean off leaf mulch and reduce wheel slip and slide, thus reducing the number and severity of wheel flats. The trains are usually formed of two RHTT vehicles 'topped and tailed' by Class 66s. On 16 October 2013, the RHTT train passes Dawlish formed of Class 66/0s Nos. 66074 and 66187 operating as the 08.45 Westbury to St Blazey.* **CJM**

Right: *One of the more unusual light power car moves to have operated along the sea wall was on 1 August 2006, when Class 47/7 No. 47714, at the time operated by Cotswold Rail and painted in Anglia livery, hauled Class 43s Nos. 43164, 43177, 43186 and 43147 as the 14.05 Bristol St Philips Marsh depot to Laira depot. The train is seen heading west approaching Rockstone bridge.* **CJM**

Above: *In May 2011, FGW formed a hybrid two-car Class 150/153 set, following a serious fire on vehicle No. 52221 of Class 150/2 No. 150221 at Laira depot. The temporary set was formed of 150/2 vehicle No. 57221 and Class 153 No. 153369. The '153' received some electrical modifications and the removal of its snowplough from the No. 2 end at Exeter depot, before operating to Laira for attachment to the Class 150 vehicle. The temporary set was allocated the number 153399, but when photographed on its first trip as a two-car passing Dawlish Warren on 12 May 2011, running as the 16.15 Laira to Exeter depot via Plymouth, it still carried its '153' number at one end and its '150' number at the other.* **CJM**

Below: *No, not a nasty graffiti attack, but a proper livery as applied by GBRf to Class 66/7 No. 66720. The colours were applied following a competition for a child to devise a livery for a loco! On 21 July 2012 No. 66720 is coupled on the rear of the GBRf staff outing special from Cardiff to Paignton, seen rounding the curve at Dawlish Warren. On the front of the train was preserved Class 50 No. 50044* Exeter, *which sadly failed later in the day with serious engine trouble.* **CJM**

Above: *In the 1990s the annual weed control operation in the West Country, which was carried out in either April or August, used a pair of Hunslet-Barclay Class 20/9s 'topping and tailing' of a rake of Normix-Chipman coaches and water tanks. On 26 August 1996 the train is seen on the sea wall approaching Rockstone Bridge powered by Class 20s Nos. 20901 and 20904. The train was returning from a trip over the Heathfield branch to Exeter Riverside.* **CJM**

Below: *Each year the VSOE, now the Belmond British Pullman, makes a three-day visit to the West Country working a Victoria to Truro train on a Friday and two Devon-based lunch and dinner trains on the Saturday, before returning to London on the Sunday. Considering the cost, these trains seem to be well loaded. On 27 April 2014 'Royal' Class 67 No. 67006* Royal Sovereign *and EWS-liveried No. 67024 emerge from Kennaway Tunnel forming train 1Z83, the 12.20 Truro to London Victoria. On this day the sea wall route was closed for maintenance, but special dispensation was given to allow the VSOE to pass.* **CJM**

Right: *One of the more interesting trains to be found lurking around the sea wall was this colourful sight of purple and yellow Class 56 No. 56312* Artemis, *Colas track machine vehicles Nos. DR76601, DR92440 and DR92377 and Colas Rail Freight Class 47/7 No. 47739 on the rear. The train, catching the first rays of winter sun on 20 January 2011, is running as 6Z76, the 07.35 Tavistock Junction to the Plasser Works at West Ealing, seen between Kennaway Tunnel and Dawlish station.* **CJM**

Below: *On 11 September 2007 a rake of fully refurbished First Great Western Mk3 HST stock was transferred back to Laira depot for return to service. The GBRf transit move was powered by black-liveried Class 66/7 No. 66709* Joseph Arnold Davies *adorned with Medite branding. The train, seen crossing Cockwood Harbour, operated as 5Z91, the 12.00 Bombardier Derby to Laira and was formed of barrier car No. 5740, a Mk2d TSO, HST vehicles 41037, 41038, 42343, 42292, 42055, 42056, 44018, with barrier No. 9481 on the rear.* **CJM**

Right: *Even before the major sea wall problems of early 2014, the cliff face on the section between Teignmouth and Parsons Tunnel had given cause for concern with major instability issues. On 29 November 2012 a significant rock fall between Parsons Tunnel and Sprey Point required the operation of a special train to clear rock and soil from the line. Freightliner Class 66/5 No. 66547 is seen arriving on the 'down' line opposite the slip with train 6Z23, the 22.23 (of 29 November) Crewe Basford Hall to Teignmouth, arriving at the worksite the following morning, 30 November, formed of 20 JNA wagons.* **Antony Christie**

The 2014 Sea Wall Collapse

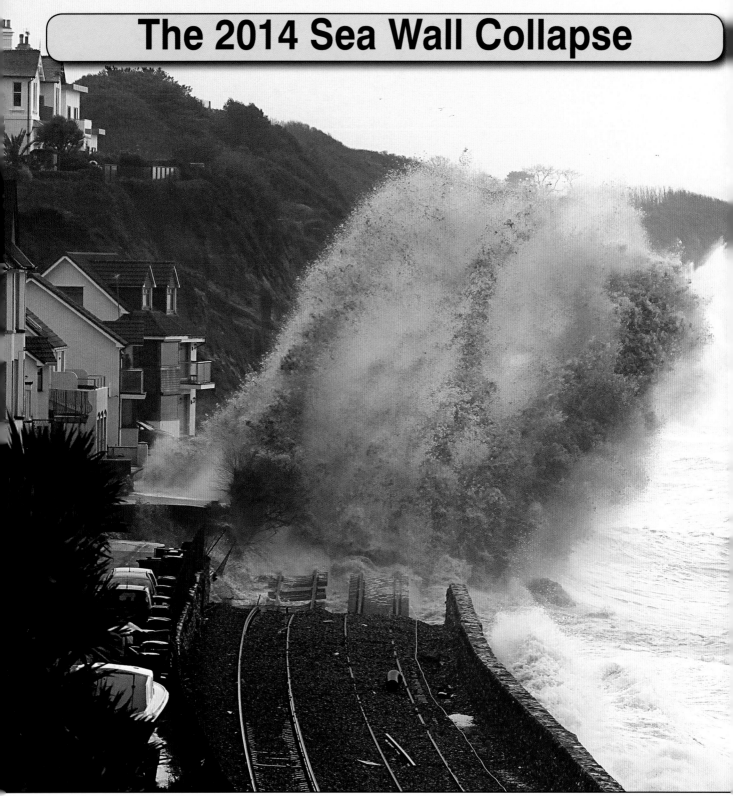

Above: *Dawlish, together with most of the West Country, was battered by the worst storm since 2007 on 4/5 February 2014. Network Rail was warned of the impending storm and ceased running trains at 15.15 on 4 February, and six hours later huge destruction was reported on the entire route from Dawlish Warren through to Teignmouth. The most serious damage was around Riviera Terrace, Dawlish, where some 265ft (80m) of the railway and sea wall had totally collapsed into the sea, dragging a road and buildings with it. Huge sections of the sea wall walkway were also destroyed, as was most of the 'down' platform at Dawlish station. The storm continued for much of 5 February with repairs starting the following day. These were progressing well, until a further massive storm struck on 14 February, ripping away another 65ft (20m) of the sea wall and line around Riviera Terrace and wrecking the previous week's repairs. A massive restoration project was then instigated with contractors Bam and Amco awarded the restoration contract, who together with Network Rail, deployed in excess of 300 staff working around the clock*

seven days a week to make repairs. The restoration saw a temporary 'wall' built using shipping containers placed adjacent to the main damage, enabling rebuilding to take place behind. A massive new section consisting of 6,000 tonnes of concrete and 150 tonnes of steel was built to bridge the gap, onto which concrete 'L' sections were fixed. Work progressed with new track, ballast, the reconstruction of the 'down' platform at Dawlish and repairs to the sea wall walkway, enabling engineering trains to start reaching the site on 18 March, to facilitate delivery of new ballast and materials. Around the clock working continued until 23.00 on Thursday 3 April, when the railway was handed back to the operators, allowing trains to start running at 00.01 on 4 April. The ceremonial re-opening of the line took place on 4 April when Prime Minister David Cameron visited the town to officially re-open the railway, thank the staff involved in the restoration project and announce 'The West is Back Open for Business'. This was the scene on 5 February with the sea still lashing into the land, tearing out the fabric of the sea wall and house foundations. **Kevin Wills**

Above: *The sight that residents of Dawlish never thought they would see: the iconic sea wall gone and waves lashing against the houses, ripping apart the road and trapping vehicles the other side of the massive growing hole. Taken early on 5 February, the railway and Sea Wall are still being impacted, the rails hang in the crater-like hole and what was a few hours earlier a road, on the left, is now a huge void.* **Kevin Wills**

Below: *Recorded at 10.15 on the morning of 5 February 2014, this is the view looking down at Marine Parade from Lea Mount. The railway is totally engulfed in water as is much of the road, while a large section of the steel fence along the railway has been torn away.* **Helen Shaw**

Above: *By the afternoon of 5 February, the wind had largely dropped and it was low tide, and thus people could start to inspect the damage. Before the authorities closed the walkway and the beach, this was the view taken from the beach at 15.30 on 5 February looking up towards Riviera Terrace, showing where the wall had been completely ripped away at the point of the lower walkway. If the storm had continued for any longer period, it is highly likely that the houses to the rear would have been washed away.*
Antony Christie

Left Middle: *Recorded by a local resident from the front of his property looking towards Rockstone Bridge and Dawlish Warren on 5 February, the gaping hole can clearly be seen, with the track bed behind the hole being a mass of destruction, with water, rocks, sections of the walkway wall and debris covering the line. This image was recorded just before Network Rail arrived and cut down the hanging tracks.* **David Lesser**

Left Below: *Within hours, Network Rail and contractors arrived to start a recovery operation. After the hanging rails were removed and the site made safe, it was agreed to build a temporary container wall in front of the main break to provide some defence from forecast high tides. Containers were obtained from Southampton, delivered to Dawlish Warren by road and then trolleyed along the wall and craned into position. Once on the walkway, holes were cut in the top and the containers filled with stones and rocks to give them weight and robustness.*
David Lesser

Britain's Scenic Railways Dawlish - The Railway from Exeter to Newton Abbot

Right Top: *While the main attention of the sea wall damage was in the area of Riviera Terrace and the main wash-out, serious damage was caused and continued to be caused in other areas, one being the breakwater protecting Boat Cove, Dawlish. This was damaged in both the 4/5 and 14 February storms. Just before dusk on 14 February this was the breakwater being buffeted; before the evening was over the waves were almost twice this height.* **CJM**

Right Middle: *Where do you start to clear up this mess? That was the question asked by the senior Network Rail engineers on the morning of 15 February, when the results of the second storm were being evaluated. 24 hours before this area was almost clear of loose ballast, but the pounding on 14 February made it look more like a bomb site. Viewed from Lea Mount looking down to King's Walk and Marine Parade on 15 February, much of the ballast had been scattered, the between-rail fibreglass panels washed away and huge damage caused to King's Walk.* **CJM**

Right Below: *The massive impact of the waves landing on the railway line swept much of the track bed ballast into Marine Parade, making it dangerous to walk and drive. Mechanical plant had to be brought in to scoop up the ballast and return it to the rail bed after the first storm, as seen here on 11 February. After the second storm the level of ballast was higher, and Network Rail hired in a huge vacuum sucker from the CrossRail project in London to clear the street.* **CJM**

Above: *Taken at the height of the second storm on 14 February, this was the view at 19.00 from the author's window. It was quite obvious during the afternoon that trouble was brewing and that further damage was going to be caused. Five hours before high tide the water was encroaching on the railway such that it would have had to stop running and by 18.00 Marine Parade started to fill with water, and the drains could not cope with the levels of liquid. At this point the only thing was to sit it out and see how bad it actually got. As the water built up, it spread further across the road and eventually entered the ground floor of some properties, as well as flooding cars.* **CJM**

Filmstrip Left: *Various views of the damage and recovery operations in Marine Parade after the second storm, showing the road awash with ballast, damaged seats, cleaning up the ballast and trying to remove the damaged sections of King's Walk. All:* **CJM**

Below: *This view looking along Marine Parade towards Dawlish station was taken at 20.00 on 14 February; at this time the road was 60% flooded and it was impossible to walk down. One amazing thing is that the street lighting remained on and none of the properties lost any services.* **CJM**

Above: *The morning after the storm on 15 February 2014: total destruction, ballast thrown everywhere, a trolley is derailed and the line is covered in debris, and much of the fence on the sea side is buckled.* **CJM**

Below: *Soon after 16.00 on 14 February 2014, the ballast bags placed on the fibreglass panels to hold them down are being battered and the fence on the sea side of the line is already twisted by the huge impact of the sea.* **CJM**

AMCOrail

COASTAL FOOTPATH CLOSED BETWEEN COASTGUARD FOOTBRIDGE AND ROCKSTONE FOOTBRIDGE

Left: *Recovery gets under way. While huge teams of men, drafted in from all over the country, worked on the main 'hole' in the sea wall, even more men were deployed in the lesser damaged areas, all reporting to a central command base set up at Dawlish Warren. Massive use was made of road-rail vehicles which could gain access to the tracks in many locations, as obviously with the gap in the line it was not possible to bring in any rail vehicles. A TXM Plant road-rail vehicle is seen collecting together the previously used fibreglass-infills to reduce ballast wash outs between Dawlish station and Kennaway Tunnel. These were later craned over the fence and taken away by road for disposal. The ballast in the area is now glued.* **CJM**

Right: *The major damage to King's Walk, which could have destabilised the actual sea wall and railway, needed huge amounts of concrete to be pumped into under-track voids. As it was not possible to take cement trucks onto the beach, a massive cement pump truck was parked in Marine Parade into which cement was poured and then pumped over the line to the required area. Most of the cement was provided by local firm Glendinning. At the same time as the pumping operation, a road-rail vehicle is delivering new sleepers to replace those seriously damaged in the storm.* **CJM**

Left: *Working space was very limited and, with so many different operations on-going at the same time, some work either had to be done in the road or in track-side areas between the tunnels. The short rail sections, eventually used to bridge the gap by the major hole, were fabricated between the tunnels, using sleepers delivered and craned onto trolley wagons in Marine Parade and using old rail sections recovered from the site. On 21 March 2014 ten sections are slowly taken to near the main work site for installation of sleepers; the rails were then removed and continuous welded rail installed. The pile of earth in the foreground was from cliff work on Lea Mount where the heavy rain and water caused a risk of a cliff fall.* **CJM**

Right: *Network Rail delivered some 300 new concrete sleepers by road to Marine Parade, which were lifted over the fence one by one and stored on the down line just short of Kennaway Tunnel until staff were ready to form the new track sections between the tunnels.* **CJM**

Left: *The Freightliner containers placed on the lower walkway to protect the main hole and then the reconstruction works are seen from the Coastguards Bridge just after the line was re-opened in April 2014. The steel steps were erected to provide a walkway for workers. This is the section which has now been rebuilt to the full height and opened to the public in summer 2015. During the period of reconstruction of the wall in February-April 2014, Network Rail installed a live web-cam on their website so people could watch the progress of the work. This is just visible on the top left of this picture.* **CJM**

Right: *Network Rail were lucky that when the sea wall collapsed, one track machine, No. DR75406 Eric Machell, was west of the problem area and was, after a couple of weeks, brought forward to Dawlish and then stabled in Kennaway Tunnel, being used to return the 'down' line to running condition. As the major land slip at Teignmouth took place after the tamper arrived in Dawlish, it was not possible to cross the machine to the 'up' line until after the wash-out at Sea Lawn Terrace was reconnected. On 17 March 2014, the machine is seen working near Kennaway Tunnel, while a road-rail ballast brusher works on the 'up' line.* **CJM**

Left: *The concrete 'L' sections used to form the new sea wall in the main collapse area by Sea Lawn Terrace were fabricated away from site and delivered by road to Dawlish station car park, from where they were mounted on a rail trolley and wheeled to site. Two different designs of 'L' section were formed, tall and short, used for either the sea or land side of the track formation. Short 'L' sections are seen stored in the car park on 1 March 2014.* **CJM**

Right: *A Volker Rail road-rail vehicle lifts one of the short 'L' sections to transport it to a rail trolley on 4 March 2014.* **CJM**

Left: *With Dawlish station and car park closed for normal use, the station car park became a major work site and store ground for materials, especially those delivered by road, which could be reversed directly into the car park for off-loading. The car park also housed the staff amenities and a canteen. The downside platform was a separate work site to allow rebuilding and while the station was closed it was agreed to carry out other refurbishment work including a new roof.* **CJM**

Right: *Heavy duty Volker Rail road-rail vehicle No. RRC13203 lowers one of the tall 'L' sections onto a trolley on 13 March 2014 which was then pushed into the worksite by a Total Rail Solutions vehicle. At the Exeter end of the station car park, a temporary railing apron was built for the road-rail vehicles* **CJM**

Left: *The 'down' or westbound platform at Dawlish was very seriously damaged in the storm, with virtually its entire length of wooden decking and back fence destroyed. A major rebuilding operation was undertaken using the same wooden-style construction with modern concrete edge coping stones. The new wooden framework is seen in an advanced stage awaiting the top decking.* **CJM**

Right: *Specialist timber contractors were brought in to rebuild the wood frame for the platform, which required joining in with the existing hardwood uprights. Special scaffolds were also erected on the walkway below to provide a safe working platform for staff.* **CJM**

Filmstrip Above: *During the storm all but three of the council-owned beach huts on the path leading to Coryton Cove and beach were destroyed, with new ones provided by a Cornish timber merchant; the 'flat packs' and assembled huts are shown. The damaged Boat Cove breakwater is seen before repairs started. Some of the 'new' beach huts were destroyed in an arson attach in September 2015.* **CJM**

Left Upper: *The condition of the cliff at Teignmouth gave serious concern, and it was decided to spray and inject water into the cliff to induce a rock slide which could be cleaned up and the embankment stabilised. The fire service provided several high-output pumps which had to be manhandled from Marine Parade to near Sprey Point. One of the Volker Rail road-railers struggles to lift one of the pumps over the fence and onto a road-rail trailer.* **CJM**

Left Below: *Part of the final restoration work before trains could run was the total replacement of the steel fence on the sea side of the railway between the Colonnade Viaduct and Kennaway Tunnel. On 26 March 2014 the old sections are cut down.* **CJM**

Britain's Scenic Railways Dawlish - The Railway from Exeter to Newton Abbot

Right: *As normal track machines could not reach the worksite west of Rockstone on the sea wall until late March, various 'heads' fitted to road-rail machines were used; these including tamping and ballast brushes, the latter generating a huge amount of dust. After the tamping head has been used the residual ballast is brushed off the 'up' line, close to Kennaway Tunnel.* **CJM**

Left: *The delivery of track ballast to the worksite was also very difficult, with no rail connection; this required hundreds of tonnes of ballast to be delivered by road to various access points in bags and then transferred by trolley to the required area. A double-section truck is being unloaded from the footpath at the west end of Marine Parade onto the embankment.* **CJM**

Right: *The damage to the Boat Cove breakwater was quite major with several of the large stone blocks washed away. Repairs were carried out by pinning and an application of 'spraycrete'; no actual new stones were fitted. Work on this, as in many areas of the sea wall, could only be undertaken at low tide, which meant that in some weeks only a few hours of work could be done each day.* **CJM**

This Page: *The first train to operate west of Exeter St Davids after the afternoon of 4 February 2015 was Colas Rail Freight-powered train 6Z70, the 11.20 Westbury to Dawlish Warren ballast train, on 18 March 2015. The train was 'topped and tailed' by brand new Class 70s Nos. 70802 and 70803. In the view above, travelling at walking pace, the train crosses Cockwood Harbour. The image left shows the rear of the train approaching Eastdon, while the view below shows the train stabled in the 'down' loop line at Dawlish Warren, where it remained until after nightfall when it worked up to the work site on the sea wall. All:* **CJM**

Above: *With the new fence being erected between the railway and King's Walk, and in near perfect photographic light, 'top and tail' Class 70s Nos. 70803 and 70801 proceed at walking pace away from Kennaway Tunnel on 1 April 2014 and head through Dawlish station and the main sea wall work site with train 6C71, the 08.50 Teignmouth to Westbury, which had been involved in work on the Teignmouth cliff stablisation and track renewal work.* **CJM**

Below: *In the few days prior to the line being re-opened on 4 April 2014, a number of mainly Class 66 and 70-powered works trains operated to Teignmouth, where in addition to the cliff work the track in the area of the cliff collapse had to be totally relaid. On 29 March 2014, Class 70 No. 70803 is seen with a ballast train stabled at Polly Steps, adjacent to the Port of Teignmouth.* **CJM**

Above: *After agreement was reached to raise the level of the lower section of the sea wall walkway between Dawlish and Rockstone Bridge to full height, Amco contracted Teign Maritime Services and hired the* Haven Seariser 4 *to act as a support rig. After several weeks of preparatory work in the Port of Teignmouth this was towed round to Dawlish on 6 September 2014 by tug* MTS Indus. *The flotilla is seen approaching Dawlish.* **CJM**

Left: *In January 2015 a second smaller support rig was brought to Dawlish for the start of the work to lower pre-formed 'L' sections onto the existing lower walkway to raise its height. With its crane jib lifting an 'L' section into position, Class 143s Nos. 143611 and 143619 pass by forming train 2F21, the 10.21 Paignton to Exmouth, on 16 January 2015.* **CJM**

Right Top: *A daytime FGW 'Night Riviera' service passes the sea wall height-raising work site on 24 November 2014. DRS Class 57/3 No. 57310* Pride of Cumbria *heads east powering train 5A40, the 10.55 Plymouth to Paddington. This loco and train should have formed the previous evening's Penzance to Paddington, but failed and thus had to operate in the daytime when the loco had been repaired, allowing it to be in London for the evening's westbound service. The new concrete wall sections can clearly be seen in this illustration; these are faced with a stone pattern and in time it is hoped they will weather down to the colour of the older sections.* **CJM**

Right Bottom: *By 1 March 2015 most of the large 'L' sections forming the raised section of the new sea wall were in position and the second support barge was returned to Teignmouth. The new 'trough' which had been formed was then filled with liquid cement, pumped down to the worksite from the Exeter Road. Also, special angled sections were inserted to bridge the join between the new and existing wall sections. A two-car Class 153 set heads west with the 12.20 Exeter St Davids to Penzance.* **CJM**

Britain's Scenic Railways Dawlish - The Railway from Exeter to Newton Abbot

Above: At midnight on 3 April 2014 the sea wall and the line from Exeter to Newton Abbot was re-opened, and a few minutes later the first two empty stock trains traversed the line. The first passenger train to call at Dawlish was the 05.34 Exeter St Davids to Paignton led by Class 143 No. 143611, which is seen arriving at Dawlish station to be greeted by photographers and a film crew. **CJM**

Left: During the morning of re-opening day, Prime Minister David Cameron visited the town to thank the 'orange army' for their efforts in getting repairs complete to return a rail service. **CJM**

Below: On 14 August 2015 came the official opening of the new raised walkway, replacing the lower section in front of Sea Lawn Terrace. The opening was performed by the Mayor of Dawlish, Cllr Howard Almond, Mayor of Dawlish, and Angela Fenne, Deputy Mayor, after 555 days of closure. Both: **CJM**

Above: *The special Dartmoor Brewery 'Dawlish on Track' beer pump clip.*

Right Top: *To mark the catastrophic events of February 2014 and the recovery of the railway, TRC Publishing produced this special edition poster which was available in local shops and businesses in the town.*

Right & Below: *On 6 September 2014, Exeter and East Devon CAMRA visited Dawlish to celebrate the re-opening of the railway. During closure, local pubs and South West brewers suffered significant disruption to their business. Dartmoor Brewery produced a special brew in honour of this event called 'Dawlish on Track' which was available for a short time in a few local pubs. The beer was described by Dartmoor 'as a delightful deep bodied golden beer inspired by the golden age of steam and beautiful sands of the Dawlish coast. At 5% ABV, it has a well rounded rich flavour with a slightly sweet and spicy after taste'. The partnership between CAMRA, FGW and Dartmoor Brewery was marked by a special photo shoot at Dawlish station, followed by a visit to the Marine Tavern to sample the new beer and others. The Marine Tavern, the closest pub to the sea wall, escaped flooding during the great storm, but was affected by serious access problems from the street for some time after. In the bottom right picture landlord Andy Sharples pulls the first pint of the new brew at 'the MT'. All:* **CJM**

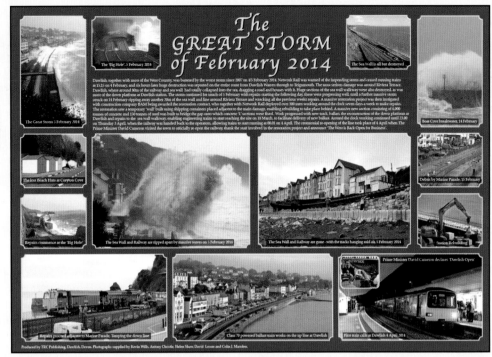

Options for a Sea Wall Diversion

Following the February 2014 exceptional weather, leading to the catastrophic destruction of part of the Dawlish sea wall and subsequent blockage of the line, rail services were suspended for eight weeks, with passengers using replacement road services. Freight traffic was transferred to road or used alternative locations to the east of the blockage.

The cost to the rail industry in terms of lost revenue and disruption is estimated at between £40-£45 million, including the cost of repairs and the compensation to passenger and freight operators.

The wider cost resulting from the storm damage and line closure is much harder to cost; what is known is that prior to the blockage, the average number of rail journeys along the sea wall daily (Monday-Friday) was 12,500.

As a result of the February 2014 storms and wash-out, there was huge public demand for a more robust rail route to be either built or re-opened to avoid the Dawlish-Teignmouth sea wall section, as a means to safeguard train services to and from the South West peninsula in the event of future storms.

In collaboration with stakeholders, Network Rail commissioned a study to look at sustainable routes between Exeter and Plymouth as part of its long-term planning process. The report looked at a sustainable route including technical feasibility, safe operation and maintenance, resilience against severe weather, the ability to accommodate forecast demand, value for money and a journey time similar to (or better than) that of 2014.

Five broad options were put forward.

1. - The Base Case of maintaining the existing railway.

2. - Strengthening the existing railway.

3. - Alternative Route A This would see the reinstatement of the original London & South Western Railway (L&SWR) route, with a modern double-track line constructed on the alignment of the former L&SWR route from Exeter to Plymouth. Tracks remain from Exeter (Cowley Bridge) to Meldon Quarry and from Bere Alston to Plymouth, but these would require upgrading. The 'new' line between Meldon Quarry and Bere Alston would need to be built.

4. - Alternative Route B This would use the original Great Western Railway (GWR) 'Teign Valley' line, building a modern double-track railway on the original alignment linking Exeter St Thomas with Newton Abbot via Christow and Heathfield. The junction still exists at Exeter St Thomas feeding an industrial spur and at the west end the freight- only line is still present from Newton Abbot to Heathfield.

5. - Alternative Routes C1 - C5 This option would see a new double-track railway built inland, bypassing the vulnerable sections of the present route between Exeter and Newton Abbot. Several potential routes have been put forward, identified as C1-C5 by Network Rail; these consist of

C1 - A twin-track route from Alphington to Ware Barton; this is the most direct route and would mostly be in a tunnel.

C2 - A twin-track route from Exminster to Ware Barton – a broad western alignment of which 66 % would be in tunnels.

C3 - A twin-track line from Exminster to Ware Barton, taking a more easterly alignment, reducing the length of tunnelling.

C4 - A twin-track line from Exminster to a point near Bishopsteignton, taking an easterly alignment, with reduced length of new construction.

C5 - A twin-track line from east of Dawlish Warren to

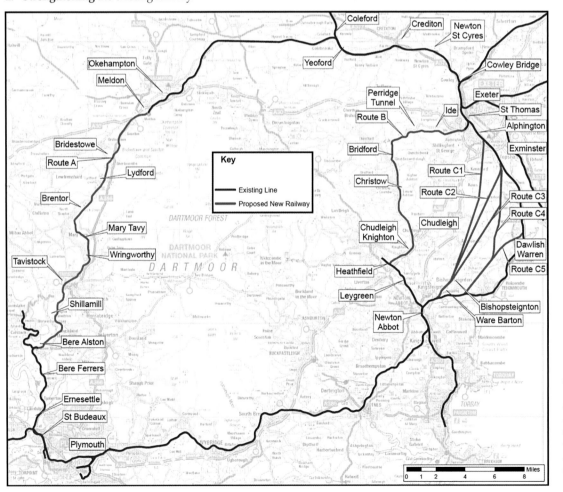

Left: Options for a diversionary or new routes to avoid the risk of further sea wall collapses. Lines coloured red are 'new' or replacement railways which would have to be built. Details of the routes are described in the text.
Network Rail

Right: *Meldon Viaduct, built in 1871 to carry the London & South Western Railway across the West Okement River at Meldon (near Okehampton) on Dartmoor, Devon. The structure is 541ft (165m) in length and is 151ft (46m) in height. This has been identified as not suitable for renovation for future use and a new structure would have to be built if this route option was furthered.* **CJM**

Below: *FGW Class 153 No. 153368 arrives at Meldon with a service from Exeter.* **CJM**

Bishopsteignton; this is the shortest length of new line.

The Options in detail

Option 1. The Base Case - this maintains the existing railway. Before the storms of February 2014, the typical expenditure on sea wall works was £800,000 per annum covering sea wall and cliff maintenance. Around every five years, £5m was spent on recovery from incidents such as a cliff collapse.

The repair works from the 2014 storm and wash-out have been expensive, with an estimated cost of £24 million. This includes repair of the sea wall, restoration of track and signalling, repairs to Dawlish station and cliff work.

During the current five-year Network Rail Control Period (CP5) covering 2014-2019, Network Rail is implementing several schemes aimed at increasing the resilience of the line; this includes a section of the Dawlish Sea Wall being strengthened adjoining the stretch rebuilt following the 2014 collapse, costing around £8 million.

Network Rail have set aside a further £5 million to be spent between 2019 and 2024 on extended maintenance, work to reduce rock falls and repairs to or building new tunnel portals.

Option 2. Strengthening the existing line - this would see a comprehensive programme of work to reduce the potential for environmental and climactic events to disrupt the railway,and would improve the ability of the infrastructure to recover from events. Fine details have yet to be confirmed, but are likely to include strengthening the sea wall and raising its parapet between Dawlish and Teignmouth to offset high tides, waves and sea spray; the installation of rock armour against the seawall for protection; the creation of an offshore rock armour berm parallel to thesea wall to reduce the impact of high tides and waves; the strengthening of signalling and infrastructure to protect against water ingress.and improvements to land drainage.

It would also deal with ongoing cliff instability by soil nailing and rock bolting to strengthen cliffs, and installation of netting to reduce falling rocks and surface soil failures on high and steep cliff areas; construction of retaining walls to contain high risk cliff falls from encroaching on the railway; installation of improved drainage and the regrading of cliff profile to reduce risk of rock falls. The timescale for these works would be between four and five years and would cost between £398 and £659 million.

Option 3. Alternative Route A The L&SWR line from Meldon to Bere Alston. If this option went ahead, it would use the original L&SWR alignment. A double-track railway would be provided for the whole length.

The line leaves the West of England main line at Cowley Bridge Junction and follows the Barnstaple line to Yeoford. At Coleford Junction the line diverges westward to follow the presently privately-owned line via Okehampton to Meldon Quarry.

The existing Meldon Viaduct, a 165 metre long and 46 metre high listed structure south of Meldon quarry, is too badly deteriorated for re-use. A new structure would be required, and would have to be adjacent to the existing viaduct.

From Meldon to Bere Alston, the dismantled line would need to be rebuilt. Many structures have been removed and the trackbed has been sold. In some places the trackbed has been lost under agriculture and, in a number of places, built upon. This includes West Devon Borough Council offices, an NHS clinic and housing developments, all of which would have to be torn down. In addition, long sections of the route have been built into a cycleway.

Currently, Devon County Council is developing a project to bring the five miles from Bere Alston to Tavistock back into use as a single-track railway. This section, together with the existing line from Bere Alston to St. Budeaux, would be re-doubled.

Compared to a newly constructed railway, this option would pose a number of issues for maintenance, and the route would not meet current maintenance clearance standards. Some sections would only be maintainable outside traffic hours.

If the route was to be electrified, it would require major work to increase clearances at bridges over the railway.

Network Rail research shows that the journey from Exeter St Davids to Plymouth by way of this route for a Class 220/221 set would be 53 minutes (non- stop), compared to 49 minutes via Dawlish. However, two train reversals add at least a further 10 to 14 minutes to a through journey via Meldon.

Even with this route option, if the line through Dawlish-

Teignmouth was closed, a replacement bus services would be required between Exeter and Newton Abbot. A shuttle train service would continue to operate between Newton Abbot and Paignton/Plymouth.

If this diversionary route was built, it has to be assumed that a regular local service would be operated (but this would not be a condition of its building), with through trains only diverted when required. An option would exist for a small number of trains to be operated via Okehampton in order that drivers retain familiarity with the route. The projected time for a local stopping service between Exeter and Plymouth has been assessed as approximately 75 minutes, based on the traction performance of a Class 165 calling at Crediton, Okehampton, Tavistock, Bere Alston, Bere Ferrers, St Budeaux Victoria Road, Keyham, Dockyard and Devonport.

The cost of this option is estimated at £875 million.

Option 4. Alternative Route B - Rebuilding the former Teign Valley Railway.

This route diverges from the GW main line at City Basin Junction, south of Exeter St Thomas. The original line was single track and the route would have to be widened throughout to accommodate a double-track railway.

The route would use the short freight branch through Marsh Barton industrial estate, which is all that remains of the northern end of the line. It then follows the course of the former railway over a supermarket car park on a viaduct and adjacent to a new housing development at Alphington.

This route would require major work to the A30 road, which is a major commuter route into Exeter. The original railway route has been lost under a road junction and a new alignment would be required. The former alignment can be regained at Ide, although the station site is now occupied by a housing development.

Beyond Ide, the line would follow the former alignment. However, Perridge Tunnel has partially collapsed. As both Perridge and Culver tunnels would require enlarging for double track, it is likely to be more practical to provide a new 1.5km tunnel.

This option would also require reinstating across farmland where the rail formation has been removed. New sections of route would also be required where the alignment is now being used by a road at Trusham Quarry and between Chudleigh and Chudleigh

Dawlish-Teignmouth route major closures due to wash outs and cliff falls	
Winter 1846	Closed for three days.
Winter 1852	Closed for seven days.
Winter 1853	Closed for three days.
February 1855	Closed for twelve days.
October 1859	Closed for three days.
January 1869	Closed for five days.
Winter 1872/73	Four closures, lasting one day, three days, three days and one day.
March 1923	Closed for three days.
January 1930	Closed for three days.
February 1936	Closed for three days.
March 1962	Closed for part of a day, with single-line working for eight days.
February 1974	Closed for part of a day, followed by single-line working for five days.
February 1986	Closed for six days, followed by single-track working for a seven days.
January 1996	Closed for seven days, due to major damage at several points.
Winter 2000/2001	Major cliff fall, closed for several days, with damage along the length of the sea wall.
19 November 2002	Wave-driven shingle damaged passing trains.
7 January 2004	Electronic signalling system rendered inoperative by heavy seas.
27 October 2004	Damage to sea wall masonry, closed for three days.
22 September 2006	Storms caused a void beneath the track, leading to single-line working for several days.
14 December 2012	Both lines closed due to flooding.
8 April 2013	A 5mph speed limit imposed for several days on westbound track due to damage to the sea wall.
5 February 2014	Major wash-out and damage, closed for eight weeks.

Knighton. Other sections are occupied by housing, including Christow and Ashton stations.

Major problems exist with this option, and construction, including moving tunnelling machinery and removing spoil, would be difficult owing to limited road access.

All former structures would need renewing or rebuilding for a two-track railway. Former level crossings would need to be replaced by overbridges.

This option offers the lowest speeds of any option reviewed, with 45-50mph being the predominant speed. A journey time penalty of 7 minutes is estimated for Class 220/221 'Voyager' trains. Some sections have been identified for speeds up to 100mph.

Basically, even at this early stage, Network Rail consider this option as not to be sustainable. Consultants consider the estimated cost for this route is approximately £470 million.

Option 5 - Building a new railway south of Exeter to bypass Dawlish/Teignmouth; five different routes have been considered.

A new route could be designed to modern standards, although the alignment would be constrained by connections to the West of England main line. NR have said that any junctions with the West of England main line would not impose speed restrictions and be

Left: *A side view of Meldon Viaduct taken from the south side; Melton Quarry is located on the far right just out of image. If the proposition was furthered to re-open this route, a new viaduct would have to be built adjacent to this structure. This view of the viaduct was taken on 27 July 2014.*
Antony Christie

designed for a maximum speed of 125mph. All five options would include a maximum gradient of 1:150, allowing freight train operation, and would be built to accommodate electrification.

The five locations where a new line potentially could diverge from the existing railway between Exeter and Dawlish Warren are at Alphington (north of the A379 road), Exminster (either north or south of the former station), Powderham (south of the River Kenn), between Starcross and Cockwood, or between Eastdon and Dawlish Warren. At the south end, there are three locations where a new line potentially could re-join the GW main line between Teignmouth and Newton Abbot, at Bishopsteignton, east of Newton Abbot, close to Ware Barton, or at Newton Abbot, joining the Heathfield line near Teigngrace.

Initial assessment of the new railway route identified 20 possible alignments. These were refined down to five. These capture all reasonable alignments capable of a 125mph top speed and a maximum gradient of 1:150.

All routes traverse open country at the north end and in tunnel section at the south end. Short tunnels are required near the north end of some routes.

A summary of the five routes is thus.

Route C1 - would see a new route between Alphington and Ware Barton. This leaves the West of England main line south of the built-up area of Marsh Barton, crosses a flood plain, then passes under the A379 road, before entering a tunnel to bypass Exminster village. There are two more short tunnels separated by bridges over local watercourses before the line crosses the River Kenn near Pennycombe Farm. The line then runs in a tunnel to Ware Barton on the Teign estuary, rejoining the West of England main line.

This option would cost approximately £3.10 billion. The journey time between Exeter and Newton Abbot would be reduced by 5 minutes.

Route C2 - would see a new route between Exminster and Ware Barton, leaving the West of England main line north of the former Exminster station, passing under Station Road and through the former station site, passing over the flood plain west of the railway on a viaduct and turning south-west, passing under Powderham ridge in a short tunnel before crossing the Kenn valley on an embankment. The route would continue south-westerly on the surface and in a cutting before entering a tunnel all the way to Ware Barton on the Teign estuary, to rejoin the West of England main line. This option is estimated to cost approximately £2.51

billion. The journey between Exeter and Newton Abbot would be 6 minutes quicker than by way of Dawlish.

Route C3 - this would see a new railway between Exminster and Ware Barton, departing from the West of England main line at the former Exminster station and passing over the flood plain west of the main line on a viaduct. It would then pass under Powderham ridge in a short tunnel before crossing the Kenn valley on an embankment and bridges. It would pass to the west of Kenton, mainly in a cutting, with a short tunnel south-west of the village. After the tunnel the line would turn south-west, entering a tunnel throughout to Ware Barton on the Teign estuary, and rejoining the West of England main line. This option is costed at around £2.25 billion.

Route C4 - this would see a new route between Exminster and Bishopsteignton, following the same alignment as C3, leaving the West of England main line at the former Exminster station and crossing the flood plain west of the main line on a viaduct. It would pass under Powderham ridge in a short tunnel before crossing the Kenn valley on an embankment. It would then pass to the west of Kenton, in a cutting, with a tunnel south-west of the village. From there, the line would continue south before entering a tunnel under the ridge on the eastern side of Dawlish Water. It would continue in a tunnel to the north of Teignmouth, east of Bishopsteignton, before passing under the A381 and rejoining the West of England main line south of Bishopsteignton. This option is estimated to cost approximately £1.56 billion. The journey reduction time between Exeter and Newton Abbot would be 5 minutes.

Route C5 - this covers a new route between Dawlish Warren and Bishopsteignton. It would leave the West of England main line south of Eastdon, crossing the coast road and turning south-west, then west to avoid the holiday camp areas, before passing north of Shutterton bridge and crossing the A379 before turning south-west to follow a stream until entering a tunnel north-east of Langdon Road. The line would then run in a tunnel to re-join the C4 alignment to the north of Teignmouth and east of Bishopsteignton and connecting with the existing main line. This option is priced at £1.49 billion and would only offer a 3 minute journey saving between Exeter and Newton Abbot.

The above options are now open for consideration. However, looking at the costs involved and the small number of times the railway has actually been closed along the sea wall, perhaps it is better just to maintain our existing railway. ∎

Right: *Looking down at Bridestowe station from the road bridge, the original L&SWR station building, platforms and SR-design footbridge are still in situ at this well-preserved station. This station is at the Meldon end of the possible 'new' railway.*
Antony Christie

Dawlish Time	Train No.	Service	Train type	Notes	Formation
00/12	1C81	21.41 Reading-Plymouth	Parcels	MX	Class 47
00/23	1V75	13.05 Aberdeen-Plymouth	Passenger	MO	HST
00/28	6M72	22.25 St Blazey-Cliff Vale	Clay	MX	Class 47
00/47	1V64	12.45 Newcastle-Plymouth	Mail	MX	Class 47
01/26	1C86	22.15 Paddington-Plymouth	Passenger	MX	HST
01/26	1A03	22.15 Penzance-Paddington	Sleeper		Class 47
01/34	1C86	22.15 Paddington-Plymouth	Passenger	MO	HST
02/13	1V78	20.30 York-Plymouth	Passenger	MO	Class 47
02/22	6V35	17.25 Ince & Elton-Truro	Fertilizer	MO	Class 47
02/34	1C87	23.17 Paddington-Plymouth	TPO	MX	Class 47
02/53	1V69	16.39 Newcastle-Penzance	TPO	MX	Class 47
03/50	1C02	23.55 Paddington-Penzance	Sleeper		Class 47
05/10	6V41	16.30 Irvine-Burngullow	Clay	TFO	2xClass 37
05/10	5O31	04.15 Laira-Exeter St Davids	ECS		Class 47 or 50
05/12	8C48	03.50 Tavistock Junction-Exeter Riverside	Engineers	FO	Class 47
05/16	5A13	04.00 Laira Depot-Taunton	ECS		HST
05/47	5B61	04.55 Laira Depot-Exeter St Davids	ECS	MX	DMU
05/50	2C99	04.55 Laira Depot-Exeter St Davids	Staff Train	MO	DMU
05/56	5C03	05.45 Exeter St Davids-Newton Abbot	ECS		DMU
06/18	1A17	05.35 Plymouth-Paddington	Passenger		HST
06/29	1V25	21.57 Leeds-Plymouth	Mail	MX	Class 47
06.30	2B64	06.18 Newton Abbot-Barnstaple	Passenger		DMU
06/46	1A21	06.00 Plymouth-Paddington	Passenger		HST
06/53	6C30	22.03 Waterston-Heathfield	Oil	TO	2xClass 37
07.11	2C62	06.54 Exeter St Davids-Penzance	Passenger		Sprinter
07/13	1E29	06.25 Plymouth-Newcastle	Passenger		HST
07.25	2C08	07.12 Newton Abbot-Exeter St Davids	Passenger		Class 47 or 50
07/44	1A26	05.21 Penzance-Paddington	Passenger		HST
07/48	6S67	04.48 St Blazey-Mossend	Freight	MWFO	Class 37
07.55	2C12	07.12 Paignton-Exeter Central	Passenger		DMU
08/03	1V33	21.20 Glasgow Central-Plymouth	Sleeper		Class 47
08.08	2C11	07.42 Exeter St Davids-Paignton	Passenger		DMU
08/13	1S85	07.25 Plymouth-Aberdeen	Passenger		HST
08/23	1A32	07.35 Plymouth-Paddington	Passenger		HST
08.33	2C14	08.02 Paignton-Exeter Central	Passenger		DMU
08.52	2C13	08.00 Exmouth-Paignton	Passenger		DMU
09.05	1E40	08.35 Paignton-Newcastle	Passenger		HST
09/19	1A36	06.46 Penzance-Paddington	Passenger		HST
09.29	2C66	06.53 Gloucester-Penzance	Passenger		Sprinter
09.39	1M09	08.44 Plymouth-Liverpool	Passenger		Class 47
10/03	1V35	06.05 Derby-Plymouth	Passenger		Class 47
10/04	1S71	07.27 Penzance-Glasgow Central	Passenger		HST
10.12	2C68	09.40 Paignton-Bristol Temple Meads	Passenger		Sprinter
10.23	2C19	09.25 Exmouth-Paignton	Passenger		DMU
10.25	1A45	09.35 Plymouth-Paddington	Passenger		HST
10/31	1C12	07.45 Paddington-Penzance	Passenger		HST
10.45	2F10	10.12 Paignton-Exmouth	Passenger		DMU
10.50	2C21	10.30 Exeter St Davids-Paignton	Passenger		DMU
11/05	1S64	10.12 Plymouth-Edinburgh Waverley	Passenger		Class 47
11/15	1A48	08.50 Penzance-Paddington	Passenger		HST
11/25	1V38	06.05 Leeds-Plymouth	Passenger		HST
11.32	2C23	09.30 Bristol Temple Meads-Paignton	Passenger		Sprinter
11.41	2F12	11.10 Paignton-Exmouth	Passenger		DMU
11/49	6S55	09.50 Burngullow-Irvine	Clay	WO	2xClass 37
11/57	1S35	09.25 Penzance-Aberdeen	Passenger		HST
11.59	2C25	11.15 Exmouth-Paignton	Passenger		DMU
12/07	1C20	09.35 Paddington-Plymouth	Passenger		HST
12.08	2F13	11.36 Paignton-Exmouth	Passenger		DMU
12/19	1A54	09.42 Penzance-Paddington	Passenger		HST
12/48	1C28	10.35 Paddington-Penzance	Passenger		HST
12.59	1M56	12.03 Plymouth-Manchester Piccadilly	Passenger		Class 47
13.06	2C73	12.37 Paignton-Bristol Temple Meads	Passenger		Sprinter
13.11	1C29	10.50 Paddington-Paignton	Passenger		HST
13.18	1V42	08.20 Leeds-Paignton	Passenger		HST
13.26	2C28	12.55 Paignton-Exeter Central	Passenger		DMU
13/44	1E36	13.04 Plymouth-York	Passenger	FX	HST
13.51	1V46	09.18 Manchester Piccadilly-Plymouth	Passenger		Class 47
13/51	6B20	13.00 Heathfield-Briton Ferry	Oil	TO	2xClass 37
13/58	1E36	13.14 Plymouth-Newcastle	Passenger	FO	HST
14/02	1C32	11.35 Paddington-Plymouth	Passenger		HST
14/12	2C70	12.25 Bristol Temple Meads-Penzance	Passenger		Sprinter

14/22	1A61	13.35 Plymouth-Paddington	Passenger		HST
14.27	2C29	14.00 Exeter Central-Paignton	Passenger		DMU
14/33	2C77	11.45 Penzance-Bristol Temple Meads	Passenger		HST
14/41	1O40	13.55 Plymouth-Southampton	Passenger	FO	Class 47 or 50
14.46	1A65	14.20 Paignton-Paddington	Passenger		HST
15/00	1E37	14.34 Paignton-Newcastle	Passenger		HST
15/07	1C36	12.35 Paddington-Penzance	Passenger		Class 47
15/10	7C05	14.20 Exeter Riverside-Tavistock Junction	Engineers		Class 37
15.12	1V48	10.16 Liverpool Lime Street-Plymouth	Passenger		HST
15/18	1E43	14.15 Plymouth-Leeds	Mail		Class 47
15/23	1A70	12.36 Penzance-Paddington	Passenger		Class 47
15.37	2F20	15.04 Paignton-Exmouth	Passenger		DMU
15.39	2C35	14.45 Exmouth-Paignton	Passenger		DMU
15/48	1V50	08.25 Edinburgh Waverley-Penzance	Passenger		HST
16/05	6M22	12.50 Truro-Ince & Elton	Fertilizer	MO	Class 47
16.15	2C37	14.28 Bristol Temple Meads-Paignton	Passenger		Sprinter
16.20	1C40	13.35 Paddington-Penzance	Passenger	FO	Class 47
16/22	1A76	15.35 Plymouth-Paddington	Passenger		HST
16/32	1M38	15.44 Plymouth-Derby	Passenger		Class 47
16.41	2F22	16.08 Paignton-Exmouth	Passenger		DMU
16.44	2C39	15.45 Exmouth-Paignton	Passenger		DMU
16/53	1A90	12.12 Penzance-Paddington	Parcels		Class 47
16/57	1C44	14.35 Paddington-Penzance	Passenger		HST
17/06	1V52	09.44 Glasgow-Penzance	Passenger		HST
17.08	2C36	16.35 Paignton-Exeter St Davids	Passenger		DMU
17/15	1A82	14.48 Penzance-Paddington	Passenger		HST
17.33	2C84	17.04 Paignton-Bristol Temple Meads	Passenger		Sprinter
17.42	2C41	16.45 Exmouth-Paignton	Passenger		DMU
17/41	1E03	13.45 Penzance-Leeds	Parcels		Class 47
17.50	2F24	17.19 Paignton-Exmouth	Passenger		DMU
18.01	1E29	17.10 Plymouth-Leeds	Passenger		HST
18/02	1C50	15.35 Paddington-Penzance	Passenger		HST
18.11	2C43	17.15 Exmouth-Paignton	Passenger		DMU
18/19	1V56	12.06 Newcastle-Plymouth	Passenger		HST
18.38	2C45	17.45 Exmouth-Paignton	Passenger		DMU
18/43	1V57	10.52 Edinburgh-Plymouth	Passenger		Class 47
19.16	1C54	16.35 Paddington-Plymouth	Passenger		HST
19/30	1V59	09.12 Aberdeen-Plymouth	Passenger		HST
18.51	2F26	18.20 Paignton-Exmouth	Passenger		DMU
19/12	6C43	16.33 St Blazey-Exeter Riverside	Freight		Class 37
19/22	1A91	16.30 Penzance-Paddington	Passenger		HST
19.31	2C42	18.50 Paignton-Exeter St Davids	Passenger		DMU
19/54	1C60	17.35 Paddington-Penzance	Passenger		HST
19/59	6V62	10.34 Fawley-Tavistock Junction	Oil		Class 47
20.12	2C49	19.45 Exeter Central-Paignton	Passenger		DMU
20/14	5C42	20.02 Exeter St Davids-Laira	ECS		DMU
20.22	2B90	17.32 Penzance-Cardiff Central	Passenger		Sprinter
20/42	1V60	14.41 York-Plymouth	Passenger		Class 47
20/51	1C66	18.35 Paddington-Penzance	Passenger	FO	HST
21.06	2C53	20.46 Exeter St Davids-Newton Abbot	Passenger		DMU
21/12	1C66	18.35 Paddington-Plymouth	Passenger	FX	HST
21/20	1V63	15.06 Newcastle-Plymouth	Passenger	FX	HST
21/21	1C68	18.38 Paddington-Plymouth	Passenger	FO	HST
21/23	5V17	20.55 Exeter St Davids-Laira Depot	ECS		Class 47 or 50
21/27	1V63	15.06 Newcastle-Plymouth	Passenger	FO	HST
21/40	5C64	21.00 Taunton-Laira Depot	ECS		HST
21/48	1S19	21.00 Plymouth-Glasgow	Sleeper		Class 47
21/55	6C17	21.40 Exeter Riverside-St Blazey	Freight		Class 37
22/13	1C76	19.35 Paddington-Penzance	Passenger		HST
22/30	6O79	21.40 Tavistock Junction-Fawley	Oil		Class 47
22.36	2C59	22.15 Exeter St Davids-Newton Abbot	Passenger		Class 47 or 50
22/47	1E05	19.23 Penzance-Leeds	TPO		Class 47
23/07	1A01	22.13 Plymouth-Paddington	TPO		Class 47
23.12	1C82	20.35 Paddington-Plymouth	Passenger		HST
23.25	2C54	22.25 Paignton-Exeter St Davids	Passenger		DMU
23/21	5V21	23.10 Exeter St Davids-Laira Depot	ECS	FO	Class 47 or 50
23/51	5B89	23.40 Exeter St Davids-Laira Depot	ECS		DMU

Key

DMU	Diesel Multiple Unit	MX	Monday Excepted
ECS	Empty Coaching Stock	TO	Tuesday Only
FO	Friday Only	TFO	Tuesday/Friday Only
FX	Friday Excepted	ThO	Thursday Only
HST	High Speed Train	TPO	Travelling Post Office
MO	Monday Only	WO	Wednesday Only
MWFO	Monday, Wednesday, Friday Only	/	Passing time
		.	Stopping time

Dawlish Time	Train No.	Service	Operator	Notes	Formation
00.11	2E67	23.41 Paignton-Exeter St Davids	FGW		DMU
00/23	5E13	23.40 Plymouth-Exeter TMD	FGW	ECS	DMU
00/46	1A40	21.45 Penzance-Paddington	FGW	Sleeper	57+stock
04/14	6C--	21.47 Newport ADJ-St Blazey	DB-S	WO	Class 66/0
04/23	1C99	23.45 Paddington-Penzance	FGW	Sleeper	57+stock
05/24	5T01	04.51 Exeter TMD-Newton Abbot	FGW	ECS	DMU
05.55	2T02	05.34 Exeter St Davids-Paignton	FGW		DMU
05/58	1A08	05.09 Plymouth-Paddington	FGW		HST
06/09	1S37	05.20 Plymouth-Edinburgh	XC		220/221
06.20	1A75	05.30 Plymouth-Paddington	FGW		HST
06.31	2T03	06.11 Exeter St Davids-Paignton	FGW		DMU
06.33	2F05	06.03 Paignton-Exmouth	FGW		DMU
06/39	1A74	05.53 Plymouth-Paddington	FGW		HST
06.42	2C41	06.28 Exeter St Davids-Par	FGW		DMU
07.04	2F07	06.34 Paignton-Exmouth	FGW		DMU
07/10	1S39	06.25 Plymouth-Glasgow Central	XC		220/221
07.15	2C42	05.24 Bristol Temple Meads-Penzance	FGW		DMU
07.30	1M29	07.02 Paignton-Manchester Piccadilly	XC		220/221
07.38	2T05	06.43 Exmouth-Paignton	FGW		DMU
07/40	1A76	05.05 Penzance-Paddington	FGW		HST
07/44	1C11	06.34 Bristol Temple Meads-Plymouth	XC		220/221
07.50	2F09	07.11 Paignton-Exmouth	FGW		DMU
08.10	2T06	07.12 Exmouth-Paignton	FGW		DMU
08.10	1S41	07.25 Plymouth-Edinburgh	XC		220/221
08.19	1A12	07.40 Paignton-Paddington	FGW		HST
08.26	2C43	06.23 Bristol Parkway-Penzance	FGW		DMU
08/37	1A77	05.41 Penzance-Paddington	FGW		HST
08.50	2F13	08.20 Paignton-Exmouth	FGW		DMU
08.57	2T07	08.32 Exeter St James Park-Paignton	FGW		DMU
09.04	2U12	06.00 Penzance-Cardiff Central	FGW		DMU
09/12	1S43	06.28 Penzance-Glasgow Central	XC		220/221
09/19	1V41	06.42 Birmingham New Street-Paignton	XC		220/221
09.24	2T08	08.23 Exmouth-Paignton	FGW		DMU
09/44	1A78	06.45 Penzance-Paddington	FGW		HST
09/44	1C73	07.06 Paddington-Penzance	FGW		HST
09/51	1V42	06.10 Derby-Plymouth	XC		220/221
09.50	2F17	09.13 Paignton-Exmouth	FGW		DMU
10/10	1S45	09.25 Plymouth-Aberdeen	XC		220/221
10.19	2T10	09.23 Exmouth-Paignton	FGW		DMU
10/26	1C04	07.30 Paddington-Paignton	FGW		HST
10/30	2C45	10.18 Exeter St Davids-Penzance	FGW		DMU
10/36	6C28	08.30 Westbury-Hackney Yard	Colas	Q	Class 70
10.36	1M41	10.07 Paignton-Manchester Piccadilly	XC		220/221
10/40	1A16	07.41 Penzance-Paddington	FGW		HST
10.47	2C67	08.00 Cardiff Central-Paignton	FGW		DMU
10.51	2F21	10.21 Paignton-Exmouth	FGW		DMU
10/55	1V44	06.00 Leeds-Plymouth	XC		HST
11.02	2E40	10.33 Paignton-Exeter St Davids	FGW		DMU
11/10	1S47	08.28 Penzance-Glasgow Central	XC		220/221
11.18	2T11	10.23 Exmouth-Paignton	FGW		DMU
11/26	1A81	08.44 Penzance-Paddington	FGW		HST
11/36	1C76	09.06 Paddington-Plymouth	FGW		HST
11.45	2F25	11.15 Paignton-Exmouth	FGW		DMU
11/46	2C69	09.00 Cardiff Central-Plymouth	FGW		DMU
11/55	1V46	06.40 York-Plymouth	XC		HST
12.03	1A82	11.30 Paignton-Paddington	FGW		HST
12/10	1S49	11.25 Plymouth-Dundee	XC		220/21
12/21	1C77	10.06 Paddington-Penzance	FGW		HST
12.28	2T13	11.23 Exmouth-Paignton	FGW		DMU
12/35	1M49	09.40 Penzance-Manchester Piccadilly	XC		220/221
12.39	1V47	08.07 Manchester Piccadilly-Paignton	XC		220/221
12.43	2F29	12.13 Paignton-Exmouth	FGW		DMU
12/50	1A83	10.00 Penzance-Paddington	FGW		HST
12/51	1V48	06.45 Newcastle-Plymouth	XC		220/221
13/01	2T14	12.49 Exeter St Davids-Paignton	FGW		DMU
13.09	1C09	10.00 Paddington-Paignton	FGW		HST
13/12	1S51	12.25 Plymouth-Glasgow Central	XC		HST
13.20	2U20	12.48 Paignton-Cardiff Central	FGW		DMU
13.24	2T15	12.23 Exmouth-Paignton	FGW		DMU
13.38	2F33	13.08 Paignton-Exmouth	FGW		DMU
13/40	1C79	11.06 Paddington-Plymouth	FGW		HST

13/45	1A85	12.56 Plymouth-Paddington	FGW		HST
13/54	1V50	06.06 Edinburgh-Plymouth	XC		HST
14/00	6C29	13.44 Hackney Yard-Westbury	Colas		Class 70
14/12	1S53	13.25 Plymouth-Edinburgh	XC		HST
14/21	1C82	12.06 Paddington-Penzance	FGW		HST
14.28	2T17	13.23 Exmouth-Paignton	FGW		DMU
14.33	1M93	14.04 Paignton-Manchester Piccadilly	XC		220/221
14.45	1A87	14.13 Paignton-Paddington	FGW		HST
14.51	1V52	06.01 Glasgow Central-Plymouth	XC		220/221
14.51	2F37	14.21 Paignton-Exmouth	FGW		DMU
15/10	1S55	14.25 Plymouth-Edinburgh	XC		220/221
15.23	2T19	14.24 Exmouth-Paignton	FGW		DMU
15/30	1C83	13.03 Paddington-Plymouth	FGW		HST
15.43	2F41	15.13 Paignton-Exmouth	FGW		DMU
15/49	1A89	13.03 Penzance-Paddington	FGW		HST
15/54	1V54	06.32 Dundee-Plymouth	XC		HST
16/12	1E63	15.25 Plymouth-Leeds	XC		HST
16.19	2T21	15.24 Exmouth-Paignton	FGW		DMU
16.23	2P93	16.05 Exeter St Davids-Plymouth	FGW		DMU
16/31	1C84	14.06 Paddington-Penzance	FGW		HST
16.43	2F45	16.12 Paignton-Exmouth	FGW		DMU
16.48	2T22	15.53 Exmouth-Paignton	FGW		DMU
16/50	1A91	16.02 Plymouth-Paddington	FGW		HST
16/56	1V56	07.50 Glasgow Central-Plymouth	XC		220/221
17.00	2E44	16.30 Paignton-Exeter St Davids	FGW		DMU
17/10	1E67	16.25 Plymouth-Leeds	XC		220/221
17.15	2T23	16.43 Exeter St James Park-Paignton	FGW		DMU
17.27	2F47	16.57 Paignton-Exmouth	FGW		DMU
17/31	6C63	15.06 St Blazey Yard-Exeter Riverside	DB-S	ThO	Class 66/0
17/49	1A92	16.57 Plymouth-Paddington	FGW		HST
17/49	1C86	15.06 Paddington-Penzance	FGW		HST
17.55	2T24	16.53 Exmouth-Paignton	FGW		DMU
17.56	2F49	17.26 Paignton-Exmouth	FGW		DMU
17/58	1V58	09.00 Glasgow Central-Plymouth	XC		220/221
18/12	1E73	17.25 Plymouth-Leeds	XC		HST
18.12	2T25	17.45 Exeter Central-Paignton	FGW		DMU
18.22	2F51	17.52 Paignton-Exmouth	FGW		DMU
18.24	1V59	14.07 Manchester Piccadilly-Paignton	XC		220/221
18/33	1C87	16.06 Paddington-Penzance	FGW		HST
18.43	2E46	17.45 Plymouth-Exeter St Davids	FGW		DMU
18/52	1A94	15.59 Penzance-Paddington	FGW		HST
19.02	2T26	18.01 Exmouth-Paignton	FGW		DMU
19.04	2E48	18.34 Paignton-Exeter St Davids	FGW		DMU
19/10	1M83	18.25 Plymouth-Birmingham New Street	XC		220/221
19/14	0F--	19.01 Exeter Riverside-St Blazey	DB-S	ThO	Light Class 66
19.20	2M67	18.52 Paignton-Bristol Temple Meads	FGW		DMU
19/33	1C89	17.03 Paddington-Penzance	FGW		HST
19/36	2E88	16.44 Penzance-Exeter St Davids	FGW		DMU
19/54	1V62	11.00 Glasgow Central-Plymouth	XC		220/221
19.59	2T27	18.59 Exmouth-Paignton	FGW		DMU
20.07	2F55	19.37 Paignton-Exmouth	FGW		DMU
20/27	1C92	18.03 Paddington-Penzance	FGW		HST
20/31	1A35	17.39 Penzance-Paddington	FGW		HST
20/39	1M80	20.14 Paignton-Birmingham New Street	XC		220/221
20.43	1C91	17.33 Paddington-Paignton	FGW		HST
20/55	1V64	13.06 Edinburgh Waverley-Plymouth	XC		220/221
21.05	2F57	20.35 Paignton-Exmouth	FGW		DMU
21/36	1C95	19.03 Paddington-Plymouth	FGW		HST
21.49	2T29	21.22 Exeter Central-Paignton	FGW		DMU
21/55	1V66	13.00 Glasgow Central-Plymouth	XC		220/221
22/05	5C94	21.53 Exeter St Davids-Laira Depot	FGW		HST
22.19	2E89	21.25 Plymouth-Exeter St Davids	FGW		DMU
22/30	1V67	18.05 Manchester Piccadilly-Plymouth	XC		220/221
22/30	1C96	19.45 Paddington-Plymouth	FGW		HST
22/52	1V68	15.08 Edinburgh Waverley-Plymouth	XC		220/221
23.00	2E60	22.30 Paignton-Exeter St Davids	FGW		DMU
23.06	2T30	22.07 Exmouth-Paignton	FGW		DMU
23/19	1C98	20.35 Paddington-Plymouth	FGW		HST

Key

DB-S	DB-Schenker		ThO	Thursday Only
DMU	Diesel Multiple Unit		WO	Wednesday Only
ECS	Empty Coaching Stock		Q	Runs as required
FGW	First Great Western		XC	Cross Country Trains
HST	High Speed Train		/	Passing time
			.	Stopping time

Britain's Scenic Railways Dawlish - The Railway from Exeter to Newton Abbot

Viewed from Lea Mount and looking towards Dawlish station, two First Great Western High Speed Trains pass on 8 August 2009. On the left, No. 43198 brings up the rear of the 08.42 Penzance to Paddington, while on the right, No. 43155, more recently named The Red Arrows, *departs from the station leading the 08.35 Paddington to Paignton service.* **CJM**

29/9/16